The Wilder Nonprofit Field Guide to

Conducting Community Forums:
Engaging Citizens, Mobilizing Communities

by Carol Lukas and Linda Hoskins

We thank The David and Lucile Packard Foundation and the Amherst H. Wilder Foundation for support of this publication.

The Amherst H. Wilder Foundation is one of the largest and oldest endowed human service and community development organizations in the United States. Since 1906 the Wilder Foundation has been providing health and human services that help children and families grow strong, the elderly age with dignity, and the community grow in its ability to meet its own needs.

We hope you find this book helpful! Should you need additional information about our services, please contact:

Wilder Center for Communities
Amherst H. Wilder Foundation
919 Lafond Avenue
Saint Paul, MN 55104
phone 651-642-4022

The Wilder Nonprofit Field Guide series has been developed by the Wilder Publishing Center to help you and your organization find success with the daily challenges of nonprofit and community work. Other titles in this series include:

Conducting Successful Focus Groups
Crafting Effective Mission and Vision Statements
Developing Effective Teams
Fundraising on the Internet

For more information about other Wilder Foundation publications, please see the back of this book or contact:

Wilder Publishing Center
Amherst H. Wilder Foundation
919 Lafond Avenue
Saint Paul, MN 55104
phone 800-274-6024
www.wilder.org/pubs

Edited by Vincent Hyman and Judith Peacock
Text design by Kirsten Nielsen
Cover design by Rebecca Andrews

Manufactured in the United States of America
First printing, May 2003

Library of Congress Cataloging-in-Publication Data

Lukas, Carol A., 1947-
  The Wilder nonprofit field guide to conducting community forums : engaging citizens, mobilizing communities / by Carol Lukas and Linda Hoskins.
    p. cm. -- (The wilder nonprofit field guide series)
Includes bibliographical references.
  ISBN 0-940069-31-8 (pbk.)
  1. Meetings--Planning. 2. Public meetings. 3. Forums (Discussion and debate) 4. Nonprofit organizations. I. Title: Nonprofit field guide to conducting community forums. II. Hoskins, Linda, 1951- III. Title. IV. Wilder nonprofit field guide.
  AS6.L85 2003
  658.4'56--dc21
                        2003003840

About the Authors

CAROL LUKAS has more than twenty-five years of consulting and training experience with nonprofit, government, community, and private sector organizations, large networks, alliances, communities, and nonprofit capacity building efforts. She led the Wilder Foundation's Community Forums program for six years. Carol is currently director of national services for the Wilder Center for Communities in Saint Paul. She typically assists groups with strategic planning, restructuring, and collaboration, and trains nonprofit consultants. She is author of *Consulting with Nonprofits: A Practitioner's Guide* and coauthor of *Strengthening Nonprofit Performance: A Funder's Guide to Capacity Building.*

LINDA HOSKINS has designed, planned, and managed forums and events for more than twenty years, working in partnership with nonprofits, community groups, and private sector organizations. Her work includes assisting nonprofits with strategic planning, board development, and data gathering through the use of focus groups, interviews, and surveys. Linda is a consultant with the Wilder Center for Communities in Saint Paul.

WILDER CENTER FOR COMMUNITIES is committed to building the capacity of leaders and organizations to work together to improve their communities and strengthen the nonprofit sector locally, nationally, and internationally. Wilder Center for Communities provides a broad range of research, consulting, training, and publishing services, and serves as partner and coordinator for local and national capacity building initiatives.

Acknowledgments

This book is the result of many years of experimentation with community forums—the drudgery of countless forum planning meetings, endless checklists, and strained budgets, balanced by the excitement of seeing people charged up because of connections they've made or because of their renewed commitment to work in communities. We thank all of our co-sponsors, partners, and forum attendees over the years for helping us learn. We hope our mistakes were minor and our successes significant for you.

Thanks to the organizations of Minnesota Decides, who agreed to allow their story to be told in this book. Thanks also to the people who reviewed the book in draft form, including Dick Goebel, Second Harvest Food Bank; Bernadine Joselyn, Blandin Foundation; Dan Johnson, Blue Cross and Blue Shield of Minnesota Foundation; and Barb Rose, Bryan Barry, and Kate Murphy, Wilder Center for Communities, for ideas and suggestions that helped us strengthen the material.

No editor in the nonprofit sector can be as worthy of acknowledgment as Vince Hyman, who's been suggesting this book for more than seven years. He can pan gold when authors are bogged down in mud or prematurely celebrating fool's gold. He is demanding, firm, supportive, and fun to work with. We thank the Wilder Publishing Center staff: Becky Andrews, Kirsten Nielsen, Kristin Drangstveit, and especially Vince Hyman—for their wise advice, jokes, positive feedback, constructive criticism, patience, and great editing, design, and production skills during the development of this field guide.

Carol is especially grateful to her children, Brenna and Kip, who encourage her to work, speak, and write from her heart.

Linda would like to thank her husband, Jim, and children, Brian and Chris, whose lives have helped to shape and enrich hers.

Contents

for public debate on issues. Forums can ensure that the community's voice is included in decision making and increase awareness and understanding of key issues facing communities. They can generate hope and confidence in communities that are short on both, and they can help build social capital—strong relationships and connections among people.

Community forums are powerful tools for educating the public, building consensus, focusing action, and influencing policy.

Community groups—neighborhood associations, community development corporations, city planning departments, foundations, faith-based organizations, schools—hold forums for a variety of reasons. They may want to raise public awareness on an issue, garner public support, inform people of new opportunities, build consensus around an issue, change public policy, create a vision for the future, or report findings from a research study. They may want stronger relationships with their constituents or visibility for their organizations.

Whatever the motivation, groups will typically convene a planning group and then realize that all the different interests and voices involved make charting a course time-consuming and difficult. They also discover that forums are very staff-intensive. Putting together a forum is not always as simple as throwing a party, where you invite people and they show up. Successful forums require careful planning, artful design, strategic communications, careful attention to detail, and the participation of many people, often with conflicting interests.

This book discusses forums with a local reach, that is, within one community or metropolitan region. It does not address forums that convene people across large geographic areas or via technology. Many of the same principles can apply to these broad-scope forums, but different logistics, communication tools, and technology are needed, and that is the subject for another book.

This book will help readers:

- Determine if a forum is the best way to achieve their goals
- Clarify the desired outcomes for a forum
- Decide who needs to be involved
- Identify resources needed to support their forum and how to obtain those resources
- Manage the logistics of event planning and execution
- Support follow-up action
- Conduct exciting, successful events that accomplish the established goals

The Wilder Nonprofit Field Guide to Conducting Community Forums: Engaging Citizens, Mobilizing Communities is intended to help community groups—whether citizens, nonprofits, government, or business—achieve their community building goals and make good use of their scarce resources. The book is organized into five sections:

Chapter 1: Planning the Forum and Obtaining Resources helps you understand three types of forums, clarify your goals, decide whether a forum is the right vehicle to achieve your goals, develop a concept paper, recruit other sponsors and partners, and obtain financial support.

Chapter 2: Preparing for the Forum covers building the forum agenda; lining up speakers, research, and other resources; launching promotions and communications campaigns; managing logistics; and designing evaluation tools.

Chapter 3: Orchestrating the Event includes suggestions on the nuts and bolts of event management—registrations, staffing, food, facilities, handouts, equipment, and troubleshooting.

Chapter 4: Sustaining the Results suggests methods for supporting follow-up action and reporting results.

Appendices include sample documents, worksheets, and a Forum Checklist to help organize your effort and save you time, as well as references to books and web sites that might be helpful.

This book is designed for quick-and-easy access to needed information and for use in many situations—holding a one-time forum or a series of forums, conducting a forum on a shoestring or with a fully funded budget, sponsoring the forum alone or with many partners and co-sponsors, having a long planning process or convening a forum in a week or two to capitalize on a recent event. Read Types of Forums in Chapter 1 first; it will be valuable to any group planning a community forum. After reading that, you can skip around in the book and look for hints and tools to help your forum achieve maximum results. At the end of each chapter, a sidebar called Forums on a Shoestring will help those readers who need to get big results with little time or money.

Planning the Forum and Obtaining Resources

Historically, the *forum* was the marketplace or public gathering space of an ancient Roman city in which judicial and public business was conducted. More recently, forums are thought of as public meetings for open discussion of issues important to a community. Across the country forums are being used to promote responsible citizen deliberation of issues that face communities, states, and the nation. Forums are a mechanism to engage citizens and organizations, and develop a common or public voice through reflection on issues and policy choices. Forums are also often used as a vehicle for initiating larger-scale and longer-term community initiatives. Within this definition, there are endless variations on the name, purpose, and design of community forums.

Forums go by many names: symposiums, dialogues, town meetings, public affairs discussions, community meetings, learning circles, search conferences, round-tables. The important common denominator, however, is open discussion, or the opportunity to exchange ideas and opinions, learn what others think, and wrestle with choices and alternatives.

This chapter will discuss

- The three common types of forums, their goals, benefits, and pitfalls
- How to plan forums to accomplish the desired goals
- Recruiting appropriate sponsors

Types of Forums

Forums are a means to an end. What happens at a forum—brainstorming, keynote addresses, small group discussions, research reports, panel presentations, creative exercises, music, or food—helps accomplish the specific goals you are hoping to achieve.

Every forum is different, and the variety of issues covered is mind-boggling. Some examples of forums include the following:

- *Through the Eyes of a Child,* a symposium for parents and those who work with children to encourage more creative parenting and nurturing behaviors.

- *Saint Paul and Beyond: Visions and Realities,* a community-wide public affairs discussion about future challenges and opportunities for the city.

- *Creating Marketplaces,* a forum to explore creative ways for inner-city neighborhoods to build economic vitality from their cultural assets.

- *Urban Youth Achievement Forum,* for youth, parents, teachers, and youth workers to celebrate ways that high-risk urban youth succeed.

- *Housing: A Roof for Everyone,* a forum exploring how cities across the United States have forged creative solutions to the demand for affordable housing.

- *Stop Talking, Just Do It!,* a forum conducted by youth to help adults understand their experience living in a multicultural world.

- *Beyond Tolerance: A Call to Action,* a forum to mobilize the community to take action to address racism in housing and education.

- *Devolution Revolution,* a series of meetings to create new relationships between nonprofits, funders, governments, and business, and to help redefine the scale and scope of publicly funded programs serving low-income people.

Within this variety of possible topics and purposes there are three main categories of forums—*community education, community engagement,* and *community action*—distinguished by the goals they attempt to accomplish. Individual forums often try to accomplish more than one of these purposes.

Community education forums

Forums focused on educating people—citizens, parents, youth, community activists, congregation members, teachers, neighborhoods, business owners, law enforcement, and many others—are probably the most common type of forum, and the easiest to organize. Many forums accomplish an education goal even when they fall short on their engagement or action goals.

Community education forums involve disseminating information about a topic, generating information or opinions about an issue, sharing information among people, identifying best-practices examples, or building skills and capabilities to do something. Success is measured by whether or not people learn something new, and sometimes by whether or not people use the new information in their work or community.

Some of the more intriguing community education forums have focused on transferring knowledge between and among cities. Urban areas large and small across the country are facing similar challenges. City-to-city learning forums attempt to share promising practices and speed up the rate of knowledge transfer between communities. Learning about promising models being used in other communities instills hope and confidence that "we can do this too."

Community education forums involve disseminating information, generating information or opinions about an issue, sharing information among people, identifying best-practices examples, or building skills.

Community education forums can be planned and conducted fairly quickly, depending on the number of people or groups involved in planning. They are an effective way to convey information to a large number of people at one time. Cautions about this type of forum include the tendency to try to fit too many presentations into the agenda, and the tendency to leave too little time for dialogue. It can also be difficult to attract people if the agenda is filled with "talking heads." People are generally more attracted to agendas that allow for significant amounts of dialogue or an action orientation.

Community engagement forums

Community engagement forums attempt to mobilize or connect people around an issue. Many forums, whatever their primary goal, also have engagement, connection, or networking as a goal.

Community engagement forums might attempt to connect people throughout a community who are all working on a similar challenge, such as job training or increasing parent involvement in schools. By forging stronger relationships around common challenges, duplication of effort can be reduced, and new synergies discovered. Community engagement forums might also create plans for the future, or decide how to tackle new opportunities for a neighborhood or community. They can help to build consensus about priorities or direction.

Community engagement forums attempt to mobilize or connect people around an issue.

They can also serve as a vehicle for motivating new leadership and volunteer effort on issues.

Success with community engagement forums is often measured by the extent to which people feel connected with others, feel heard, learn new perspectives, and feel energized by an emerging consensus or direction. Other success indicators might be a significant number of people meeting after the forum, increased volunteer effort on a task, or a high level of engagement with a particular community issue.

People value connecting with others, and it is often easy to attract them to these forums. Participants often leave with enthusiasm and commitment to the topic. However, artful design and skilled facilitation are very important to achieve the community engagement goals.

Community action forums

Community action forums stimulate joint action on, or resolution of, an issue, or otherwise attempt to influence public policy or decisions. Community action forums might involve gathering neighborhood leaders, elected officials, and technical specialists to examine proposed city improvements or funding policy. They might convene experts and practitioners in a human services field to examine the effectiveness of current service delivery systems. A forum might educate parents about a new reading program in the public schools and equip them to start a home-based reading routine. Or a forum might invite people to learn about the needs of new immigrants and plan ways to support new immigrant families in the community. While community engagement forums focus on individual action and connections between people, the distinguishing goal of community action forums is some concrete action in the community or within a system (housing development, job training, tax policy, public schools).

Community action forums are the most difficult kind of forum to organize. They often require significant preparation—assembling research findings, preparing informational handouts, and soliciting the involvement of key decision makers. Community action forums also require follow-up, because the real measure of success is change in policy or increased action on an issue. The forum is usually just one step in a more lengthy strategy intended to result in some change in the community. Sometimes the forum is part of a planned policy strategy; at other times the policy strategy only becomes clear after significant support for an issue is expressed at a forum. Success is measured by whether or not that change in policy actually occurred.

Community action forums stimulate joint action on, or resolution of, an issue, or otherwise attempt to influence public policy or decisions.

The advantage of community action forums is that people value the opportunity to be heard on policy issues and real change can result. Three factors are critical in preparing for a community action forum:

- Involving people who can actually influence policy decisions early in the planning
- Doing sufficient homework so that people have complete and accurate information on which to base their work in the forum
- Building an infrastructure to sustain follow-up action

How the three forums relate

The boundaries between the three types of forums are not discrete. Community education forums typically focus on education—bringing information to people, or sharing information among people. Community engagement forums include this education component, but add ways to engage people with others in the community. Community action forums typically include elements of community education and community engagement, but also address the need for broader changes in communities or systems.

The relationship among the different kinds of forums is illustrated in Figure 1 on page 6.

Figure 1. Relationship among the Three Types of Forums

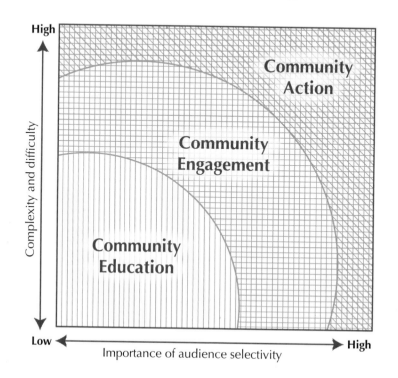

Figure 1 illustrates the relationship among the different types of forums. Progression from community education to community action forums involves increasing levels of complexity and difficulty in planning and logistics, and requires a more select audience to achieve the forum goals.

Community education forums are the easiest to plan and orchestrate; community action forums are the most difficult. With community engagement and community action forums, the difficulty or complexity increases because of three factors:

- Increasing importance of research and information preparation prior to the forum
- Increasing skills needed on the part of discussion facilitators
- Escalating importance of planning and managing post-forum activities

The importance of audience composition also increases in moving from community education to community engagement to community action. Community education forums normally require broad clusters of people who usually self-select; whether certain individuals or organizations are represented is less important. Community engagement forums require the involvement of individuals and groups who will motivate and coordinate newly engaged participants. Community action forums require the involvement of specific decision makers or influential organizations that are able to move issues to resolution.

Being clear about the goal or goals you want to achieve is the first key to holding a successful forum.

Being clear about the kind of forum you are planning—the goal or goals you want to achieve—is the first key to holding a successful forum. Later in this chapter, you will begin to set goals for your forum. At that point, Figure 1 will help you clarify your goals on the continuum of education-engagement-action.

Other benefits of forums

A forum is normally selected as a strategy to accomplish a specific goal—education, engagement, or action. Forums are typically sponsored by one or more organizations or community groups, and involve many other people and organizations. They can be highly visible events. Because of this visibility, they often bring other benefits to the sponsoring group or groups, including

- Public exposure for the sponsoring organizations and their work
- Stronger connections with the sponsors' neighborhoods or constituencies
- Increased community involvement in the sponsors' work
- New partnerships among sponsoring organizations
- Media attention to selected issues

Forum Planning

The overall process of planning a forum usually begins when an individual, a community group, a nonprofit organization, a government agency, a business group, or a collaborative is dissatisfied with a situation or wants to respond to a need in the community. If the individual or organization selects a forum as the way to make a change, they must then decide whether to convene the forum independently or to recruit others to form a planning group.

Forums convened by one organization with clear decision-making channels are fairly easy to plan and execute. Forums with multiple sponsors and multiple organizations represented on the planning team are far more complex and time-consuming. This is especially true when multiple layers of objectives and self-interest must be balanced and addressed. Despite the added complexity, a recruited planning group can bring heightened creativity, broader reach, and greater success; it may be essential to accomplishing certain goals.

If a planning group is formed, goals for the forum—usually some combination of educational, engagement, or action goals—are discussed, expanded, and established at the first meeting. The group also brainstorms possible events or facilitated activities that might help to achieve those goals. For example, a planning group's goal is to help community members better understand the Vietnamese culture. They consider asking a local acting company to present a one-act play on the topic, followed by breakout group discussions, ending the forum with a luncheon of traditional Vietnamese foods.

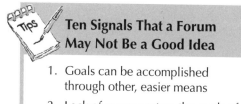

Ten Signals That a Forum May Not Be a Good Idea

1. Goals can be accomplished through other, easier means

2. Lack of agreement on the goals of the forum

3. Difficulty attracting a strong leader or facilitator for the planning effort

4. Difficulty getting participation from key constituencies

5. Too many other forums or events happening at the same time

6. Not enough lead time

7. Difficulty getting decision makers on board for a community action forum

8. Difficulty raising enough money to run the forum effectively

9. No evidence that the target audience will find the topic compelling

10. Conflict, diminishing interest, or poor attendance at planning group meetings

At the end of the first planning group meeting, one or two people take responsibility for drafting a concept paper that conveys and amplifies the goals and possible forum events. Forum planners can expect the concept paper and forum goals to grow and change as new people join the planning group. As people work to turn ideas into concrete actions, it becomes clear that forum planning is an iterative process—one in which each decision has an impact on the whole.

Whether the forum is a one-time event convened by one organization or a longer-term engagement strategy led by multiple partners, it requires careful planning, financing, promotion, and the involvement of many people to be successful.

The rest of this book outlines the main tasks that need attention when planning and conducting forums—whatever the size and scope. The sidebar Planning Group Agendas for a Streamlined Planning Process, pages 10–11, will help you create a planning process. The appendices contain additional tools and worksheets to help plan and organize forums.

The rest of this chapter will help the reader

- Establish a planning group and lead the planning group through the necessary planning steps
- Research the forum
- Select forum design elements
- Develop a timeline
- Create a budget
- Develop a concept paper
- Recruit sponsors

You can begin to use the Forum Checklist in Appendix C, page 106, as you accomplish these tasks.

Establish a planning group

As mentioned above, most organizations convene a group to plan the forum. The planning group might be just a couple of people, or it might involve representatives from many organizations.

Role

The role of the planning group varies from forum to forum, and for different types of forums. Three factors will determine the role a planning group serves for a particular forum: scope, staff support, and ownership. These factors will determine whether the group's role tends toward hands-on action or decisions and delegation.

Scope: A forum that is a one-time event, sponsored by one organization, will likely have a small planning group and a fairly efficient process. A forum that attempts to attract very broad and diverse community participation will need a large, diverse planning group and a longer planning horizon.

Staff support: When staff support is strong, the planning group can guide major decisions and leave implementation to staff. When staff support is limited, the planning group handles implementation, often working long hours and contributing volunteer labor from many organizations.

Ownership: When one organization wants to maintain control and get credit for the forum, the planning group becomes advisory to that organization. When broad ownership is desired, to ensure participation or follow-up action, the planning group needs to share decision-making authority. The planning group's precise level of authority needs to be clarified at start-up when recruiting members.

Responsibilities

Typical responsibilities of a planning group include the following:

- Decide the overall goal and design for the forum; finalize the concept paper.
- Assist in raising funds and in-kind contributions for the forum.
- Assist with development and distribution of promotional and communications materials.
- Select speakers, presenters, entertainment, and other forum activities.

Planning Group Agendas for a Streamlined Planning Process

A simple forum can be planned, with multiple sponsoring groups, in as few as four meetings if staff support is strong and fundraising isn't a problem. The following meeting agendas outline such a process. These agendas can be adapted to suit your forum situation.

Meeting 1: (two hours)
1. Make introductions.
2. Clarify purpose of meeting.
3. Describe what led to forum idea, and present brief outline of possible forum goals and design elements.
4. Record on newsprint ideas to enhance forum concept, and pros and cons of moving ahead with plans.
5. Decide whether to proceed.
6. Decide who will take the lead.
7. Decide who else to invite to participate, and how to invite them.
8. Schedule future meetings.

Between meetings:
1. Draft beginning concept paper incorporating ideas from first meeting, noting areas where additional information is needed.
2. Call additional people for planning group.
3. Send meeting notice with draft concept paper and Meeting 2 agenda.

Meeting 2: (two hours)
1. Make introductions.
2. Describe what led to forum idea, and present draft of concept paper.
3. Record on newsprint ideas to enhance forum concept.
4. Reach agreement on forum goals and overall design.
5. Identify decisions that need to be made, such as fundraising, speakers, date, location, and promotions, and assign these areas to subgroups to work on prior to the next meeting.
6. Confirm next meeting date.

- Assist at forum events as needed, helping with introductions, presentations, discussion facilitation, registration desk, setup, and cleanup.

Selection

When selecting people for the group, consider group size, representation, and expertise.

Group size: Select only as many people as you really need, and no more. The larger the group, the longer and more difficult the planning process. However, you need enough participants to generate creative ideas about your goals, audience, and design, and enough participants to generate ownership among key constituencies. Keep the group as small as possible for the early stages of planning. The group can be enlarged later as your goals become clearer and as you recruit other sponsors, funders, or partners.

Planning Group Agendas (continued)

Between meetings:
1. Revise concept paper with draft timetable for forum and send with next meeting notice.
2. Have subgroups work on assignments and prepare reports for next meeting.
3. Secure funding if needed.

Meeting 3: (three hours)
1. Clarify purpose of meeting.
2. Confirm changes made in concept paper.
3. Have subgroups report on their progress. Decide issues as needed.
4. Review draft timetable and finalize.
5. Identify tasks needing attention and assign to subgroups as appropriate (lining up speakers, developing promotional materials, handling registration process, and so forth). See Forum Checklist, page 106.
6. Confirm next meeting date.

Between meetings:
1. Make needed changes to concept paper and timeline and mail with meeting notice.
2. Have subgroups work on assignments and prepare reports for next meeting.
3. Confirm forum location, speakers, and other key resources.
4. Draft forum agenda.
5. Develop promotional materials.

Meeting 4: (three hours)
1. Clarify purpose of meeting.
2. Finalize all forum plans: name, agenda, location, promotional materials and strategy, registration process, event assignments, and so forth. Delegate responsibilities as needed.
3. Decide whether to hold a pre-forum meeting to check last-minute details and a post-forum meeting to discuss successes, failures, and impact.

Representation: The forum has a greater likelihood of success if people who will be instrumental in funding it, recruiting important audiences, or implementing changes resulting from forum discussion are part of the planning. If you hope to influence legislation, getting a legislative representative on board early will help you understand how to be successful in the lawmaking arena. If the forum focuses on parent-teacher cooperation, have both parents and teachers on the planning group. If you want to attract a corporate sponsor, adding someone well connected in the business sector is a wise strategy. Your most powerful and effective promoters will be planning group representatives. A planning group that is composed of a cross section of the community—business, nonprofit, and government—has more resources and broader reach and impact.

Many forum planners and sponsors find that the relationships forged during forum planning are at least as important an outcome as the forum itself. These relationships may carry over into other work of the sponsoring groups and may lead to future collaborations.

Expertise: Select people who understand both the subject matter and the audience you are trying to reach. You don't want to go down a wrong path because of inaccurate or incomplete information about the topic or your audience.

Leadership

Leadership of the planning group is key to its success. Select a chair who can firmly and efficiently guide the group through decision making and make sure that the many and often divergent opinions are heard. The facilitation style of the chair can make the difference between an efficient and effective planning process and one that lacks focus or stalls in midstream. The biggest leadership challenge is to find balance between hearing many ideas and opinions and maintaining momentum.

Structure

A planning group can work together on the various responsibilities, or it can divide into subgroups or task forces. When forum planning is complex or the timeline is tight, assigning tasks to subgroups is often more efficient. The risk in dividing into subgroups is that the large group often wants to rework the decisions of the subgroups, resulting in wasted time. Strong leadership and clarity about assignments and authority are critical to making subgroups efficient. Typical forum planning subgroups might focus on fundraising, lining up speakers, or marketing and promotions.

Research the forum

All three types of forums—community education, community engagement, and community action—need accurate, timely information. As mentioned earlier, community education forums disseminate information about a topic, identify best-practices examples, or build skills. Community engagement forums attempt to connect people who are all working on a similar challenge or engage people in new opportunities for a neighborhood or community. Community action forums inform or influence public policy or decisions and stimulate joint action on, or resolution of, an issue.

The kind of information needed, the way it will be presented, and the methods for collecting it vary widely from forum to forum. Because pertinent information provides the grounding for much of the work of a forum, gathering and summarizing this information will greatly influence the overall success of the forum.

Sometimes you will already have much of the information you need. Or the information may exist elsewhere in the community or another organization, such as with school districts, city planning departments, or research organizations. For each forum, you have to determine what information is needed, who has the information, and how many sources you need to ensure reliability of the data. Methods of data collection vary depending on what information is needed, the number and accessibility of sources of information, and the time and money you have available. Some of those methods can include records review, face-to-face or telephone interviews, written surveys, focus groups, and direct observation or experience. *Consulting with Nonprofits: A Practitioner's Guide*[1] by Carol Lukas has an informative chapter on gathering, analyzing, and reporting data.

To research your topic, use these questions as a guide:

1. What issue are you addressing? How can the issue be described concretely? What facts are known about it?

2. If there are differing points of view on the topic, what are they?

3. Has the community tried to address the issue before? Have other communities, neighborhoods, or cities tried to address the issue?

4. What strategies have worked or failed?

5. Who are the individuals or groups already addressing the issue?

---

[1] Carol A. Lukas, *Consulting with Nonprofits: A Practitioner's Guide* (Saint Paul, MN: Amherst H. Wilder Foundation, 1998) 37–50.

6. What assets or resources are available in the community to address the issue?

7. Who are the experts on this issue? Where can their opinions be found (Internet, library, community, or academic studies or reports)?

8. What will be the biggest barriers to addressing the issue? Who needs to be involved to tackle the barriers?

The information you gather will strengthen your case for attracting funding or sponsors, serve as a foundation for discussion or reflection at the forum, and guide action after the forum. Research is one of the most important preparation steps, and it supports creation of the most effective design for the forum.

Design the forum

Design refers to how the forum is structured to achieve the goals you've set for it. A successful design includes techniques, tools, or facilitated activities that will influence an audience's knowledge, skills, and attitudes in a way that fosters the greatest change possible.

The overall forum design is critically important. There is no one "best" design—your design will need to be tailored to fit your unique goals and audience. The design of a community education forum will be very different from the design of a community engagement or community action forum. The design for a forum process to reach youth and parents in a particular neighborhood will look very different from the design for a forum process to reach all affordable housing developers in a metropolitan area. For some forums, follow-up will be crucial; for others it will not be as important.

Consider five principles when thinking through your overall forum design.

1. **Keep your goals in front of you.** Choose each element of your forum design to help you achieve your goals. Forums have a way of getting bigger and more complex as groups of people with different interests and affiliations get excited about the plans. Avoid "forum creep." Keep asking, Will this activity or feature help us achieve our goals? Could we accomplish the same thing another way?

2. **Engage your audience early.** If you want people to be excited about the forum, and to think or act differently as a result of the forum, you have to engage them early in the planning and preparations. And you must engage them with integrity; if you ask them to join the planning group,

you need to be open to their influence, even if it means changing your ideas or plans. You also need to take the forum to your audience. If you want neighborhood people to attend, hold the planning meetings and the forum in the neighborhood. If you want businesspeople to attend, hold the meeting downtown or where businesspeople normally meet.

3. **Get accurate information about your issues.** Get facts about the issues you intend to address, and make sure the information is accurate. Your message will be more powerful, your case more compelling, if you have solid information for people. Invest in research to document what has happened related to your topic, what the current situation is, and promising approaches for the future. Prepare and distribute short briefing papers.

> **To create your forum design, you must think about the types of activities that will influence your audience's knowledge, skills, and attitudes in a way that will help achieve your goals.**

4. **Work within your resources.** Keep in mind the time you have available, the money you have, and the person-power you can devote to the forum. Assume that the forum will get more complicated and time-consuming as it gains momentum. If you have only three weeks to pull off a forum, keep the forum simple: letter or e-mail invitations, one speaker, simple food. You don't need a catered lunch to make a forum great, but you do need a welcoming atmosphere, compelling presenters, and good interaction among the participants.

5. **Be creative.** Many events and messages are competing for people's time and attention. Do something that will attract people, get them excited, and be memorable. Do it with character and style so they are proud to be part of the forum. Give people take-aways such as small plants for their home or office, a compass to signify a new direction, or a poster or note-pad printed with a sentence that captures the forum's message.

Refer to the techniques, tools, and facilitated activities listed in Appendix C, Forum Design Elements, as you begin to design your forum. More information about these and other forum design elements can be found in the resources listed in the same appendix.

Pages 16–18 are three designs drawn from actual forums that illustrate how the forum design can be created to fit specific forum goals and maximize the forum's impact. Note how the five design principles described above apply to each of these forums—a community education forum, a community engagement forum, and a community action forum.

Design for a community education forum

Name: Stop Talking, Just Do It! Youth's Perspectives on Bridging Differences

Goals: 1. Learn how youth experience racism.

2. Identify ways that the community can be more supportive of youth.

Design elements:

1. This forum was part of a forum series called Unleashing the Power of Our Community: A Public Dialogue on Race, Connections, and Commitment. Sponsors of the series included more than twenty nonprofits, businesses, and foundations committed to countering racism in the city.

2. Prior to the forum, discussion groups were held with area youth to explore their experiences with racism. Some (not all) of the youth from these sessions volunteered to share their experiences at the public forum. Members of the planning group coached the youth volunteers to prepare them to talk openly in public, and the youth met with the main speaker two hours before the forum began.

3. Aggressive recruitment was done prior to the forum to attract area youth, parents, teachers, and community members.

4. The evening forum was four hours long. It was open to the public and included dinner. The forum included:

    *   A national expert on working with high-risk youth shared his experience and research. He then hosted a "talk show" with a dozen youth volunteers. These youth reacted to his comments and shared their own very personal and moving experiences.

    *   There was a facilitated dialogue among the audience, the talk-show youth, and the main presenter.

    *   Discussion groups at each table shared their reactions and talked about how the community can be more supportive of, and involved in, the lives of youth.

    *   Reporters from each table shared the ideas that were generated.

5. A lunch forum for community leaders and educators was held the same day as the evening public forum. The guest speaker from the evening forum gave a short talk from his research and experiences working with high-risk youth. Groups at tables talked about how his experience related to what was happening in the local community.

Comments:

The primary design challenge for this forum was preparing the youth volunteers to speak for themselves on a very sensitive subject in front of a large audience, rather than having adults speak for them.

Participation goals included having at least half the audience under age twenty-one and having at least half the audience composed of people of color. These goals were reached by having youth on the planning group and by working through existing youth and community organizations and leaders.

Design for a community engagement forum

Name: A Call to Action: Rebuilding Our Neighborhood from the Inside Out

Goals: 1.   Create a vision for a stronger, healthier South End neighborhood.

2.   Get fifty previously inactive community members working to strengthen the neighborhood.

Design elements:

1.   The neighborhood community development corporation, citizen participation organization, and chamber of commerce came together determined to halt the decline of the neighborhood.

2.   An initial concept paper for the forum was used to stimulate interest and recruit co-sponsors from area schools, faith-based groups, businesses, and neighborhood clubs.

3.   The forum was promoted as a community gathering with food, music, and a serious agenda: the future of the neighborhood.

4.   The evening forum was four hours long. It was open to the public and included dinner.

5.   Preparation included development of presentations on neighborhood assets and challenges and training of small group facilitators.

6.   The forum included four sets of activities:

- Dinner, with discussion questions at each table to serve as icebreakers. An African American youth drum corps and a Cambodian storyteller entertained during dinner.
- Presentations on neighborhood assets and challenges.
- Small group visioning exercise, leading into a large group pooling of ideas and an overall vision for the neighborhood.
- Self-selected groups formed by interest in various elements of the new neighborhood vision (safety, street beautification, run-down rental properties and absentee landlords, and business development). People were asked to commit to meet after the forum to develop strategies to bring about change on their topic. People who signed up to help with follow-up were paired as "buddies" to remind each other to follow through.

7.   Interpreters and facilitators were available in four languages, in addition to English.

8.   Each of the sponsoring organizations agreed to provide leadership to at least one of the follow-up action teams.

9.   Door prizes were given, donated by sponsoring organizations and businesses.

Comments:

There were two main design challenges for this forum:

1.   Strong facilitation to move the three hundred people who attended through visioning to action planning in a short period of time. A facilitator was hired to lead the overall process and provide training for facilitators for the small group discussions. Several of the small group facilitators were bilingual to accommodate different language preferences.

2.   A very tight planning timeline. The community group got bogged down in too many ideas and behind in its schedule. It finally hired someone to facilitate the planning process and manage registration for the forum.

Design for a community action forum

Name: Minnesota Decides: A Community Blueprint for Tobacco Reduction

Goals: 1. Involve diverse audiences in the effort to reduce tobacco use and engage those who previously have not been active in the issue.

2. Obtain a strong and sustained commitment from local and state government and the private sector to reduce tobacco use, including a significant increase in the price of tobacco.

3. Develop an infrastructure to sustain and support tobacco reduction efforts.

Design elements:

1. This was a long-term effort to change policy and public behavior. Forums were one part of a broader strategy.

2. Minnesota Decides was launched with ten community forums, bringing together a cross section of people in communities across Minnesota, to discuss their thoughts and ideas on reducing tobacco use. Each forum was limited to sixty people. The forums included presentations on tobacco use trends and current tobacco control activity; a panel discussion on tobacco use and control at the local level; and discussion about what should be done to address the problem.

3. Following the forums, state and national experts were consulted to comment on the community recommendations and to add their perspectives.

4. Fifty Minnesotans from diverse organizations and backgrounds were surveyed on the key components that should be reflected in a statewide goal to reduce tobacco use.

5. The findings from the forums, experts, and surveys were brought together at a statewide summit that included two days of discussion, debate, small group work sessions, and expert presentations. The result of this summit was a set of policy recommendations for long-term tobacco reduction.

6. The findings and recommendations for Minnesota Decides are now being used in a variety of ways to sustain efforts toward the goal and to influence legislative decision making about state tobacco settlement proceeds.

Comments:

The forums and the statewide summit are classic examples of community action forums embedded in a long-term public policy strategy. They involved substantial preparation and follow-up support by the sponsoring partnership, which included six public, private, and nonprofit organizations. One main challenge at the ten forums was to limit the number of public health staff and tobacco control volunteers and broaden the base of participation. After the summit, the challenge was to focus all of the input and ideas into a compelling action plan that could be moved into the policy arena.

Develop a timeline

The forum plan needs to include a realistic timeline. A small forum, with a limited audience, led by one group or organization can be convened in four to six weeks. Six to twelve months are needed to prepare for a large forum in order to ensure broad community ownership and good attendance.

Use Worksheet 1: Forum Timeline, page 83, to help you develop a realistic timeline for your forum.

Create a budget

Even done on a shoestring, a forum can be costly, with many unexpected expenses. It is common to raise funds for a forum, whether it is part of an existing program within an organization or a new, stand-alone project. In order to raise funds to support a forum, you will need a budget itemizing both revenue sources and expenses. Most sponsors will be reluctant to contribute money without some idea of what the total forum cost is likely to be.

Revenue budget

Revenue to support forums can come from several sources. The most common, and usually the largest, source is grants from local foundations or corporations. Grant requests will be considered based on the specific goals of the forum and on the credibility and track record of the proposed sponsors or planning group. Depending on the amount being requested, the completed concept paper with budget may be adequate, or a full grant application may be required.

Other revenue sources include contributions from sponsors, either in cash or donated goods or services. Registration fees can also help to offset the cost of forums, particularly the cost of meals. (Note that the downside of registration fees is that, depending on the amount and on the target audience, they can discourage attendance.)

In-kind contributions can often be obtained just for the asking. Large local corporations with in-house creative or printing shops may donate brochure design or production if they can have their name on the brochure. Corporations may also be willing to cover the cost of the meal if they get publicity for their contribution. In-kind contributions should be represented in the revenue portion of the budget, equal to the estimated value of the in-kind contributions included in the expense budget.

Expense budget

Forum expense items will vary depending on the type of forum and how it is designed. Common expense items include staffing, space rental, food and other refreshments, speaker or moderator fees, brochure design and printing, postage, copying, and equipment rental. Other expenses might include travel and related expenses for speakers, report writing and production, translation and interpreter fees, child care, entertainment, and advertising costs.

In-kind contributions can be a significant portion of the forum budget. The value of donated staff time alone can add up. And, if money is to be raised from outside sources or a report drafted on forum outcomes, it is worthwhile to develop an operating budget that represents all costs, including costs covered by in-kind contributions. Donations from outside contributors, such as donated space, food, or printing, and contributions made by sponsors or planning committee members, such as staff time, copying, and mailing costs should be represented as expense items even though there is no cash outlay for them. Including them will give a more accurate picture of the total cost of conducting the forum.

A sample forum budget is included in Appendix A, pages 66–67.

Use Worksheet 2: Forum Budget, page 85, to help you develop a realistic budget for your forum.

Develop a concept paper

A concept paper is invaluable in recruiting sponsors for the forum, ensuring agreement on forum plans, clarifying a forum budget, and attracting funding. It is a living document, evolving as forum plans develop. Prior to the first meeting of the planning group, outline some beginning ideas for the concept paper. The outline will be useful in initiating discussion.

The concept paper usually has ten sections:

1. **Background.** Why the forum is being considered, and conditions that make the forum urgent or timely.

2. **Goals.** What the forum will accomplish, or what outcomes will result.

3. **Target audience.** Who will participate, and who will benefit from the forum.

4. **Design elements.** Major benchmark activities or events associated with the forum, and the schedule of events.

5. **Planning group.** People and their affiliations that will guide the planning process.

6. **Sponsorship.** Proposed sponsors of the event, including ideas about what sponsorship entails.

7. **Staffing.** Who will staff the forum, including support for the planning team, promotions, registration, and other logistics. One organization may have to serve as fiscal agent.

8. **Evaluation.** How the forum will be evaluated.

9. **Cost.** An operating budget for the forum, showing all expenses and direct and in-kind contributions.

10. **Funding plans.** How money and in-kind contributions will be raised, and from what sources, including sponsor contributions.

A sample concept paper is provided in Appendix A, pages 68–71.

A well written concept paper is invaluable in recruiting sponsors for the forum. Sponsors can play a variety of roles as listed in the following section.

Use Worksheet 3: Concept Paper, page 87, to help you develop your forum concept.

Recruit sponsors

Sponsoring organizations serve several important roles in forum planning and execution:

• They have expertise and connections with resource people to strengthen forum planning.

• They provide credibility and visibility to attract funding, speakers, and media attention.

• Their names and networks can attract higher attendance.

• They can provide much needed volunteer help during the planning and execution of forums.

• They can get the attention of decision makers.

• They may provide funding for the forum or follow-up activities.

As mentioned earlier, a forum can be sponsored by one organization or by many. The planning group is an obvious source of sponsors for the forum. The convening organization or planning group should think strategically about whom they want as sponsors, and what they expect of sponsors. Sponsors are often chosen based solely on their relationship with the convening organization or planning group members, or their ability to fund all or a portion of the forum. In choosing sponsors, think beyond existing affiliations to organizations that represent constituencies that you want to attract to the forum or influence after the forum. Each sponsoring organization should bring some unique strength to the table to contribute to the success of the forum. Consider potential sponsors from all sectors and segments of the community—business organizations (chambers of commerce, business associations, corporations, and neighborhood businesses), government agencies (local, county, regional, state), foundations, educational institutions (colleges, local schools), faith-based organizations.

Use Worksheet 4: Forum Sponsor, page 90, to help you formalize the commitment of sponsors. This worksheet can be tailored to suit your forum situation.

A common challenge for forum planners is determining the extent to which the forum design supports the organizational or political agendas of sponsoring members. If there are many co-sponsors, it is possible to have competing agendas, and the sponsors' agendas may vary from the community's interests. These dynamics, although never easy to resolve, can be dealt with openly and respectfully by skilled leadership.

In some cases, each sponsoring organization is expected to make a financial contribution. In other cases when funding is obtained from an independent source, sponsors are expected to provide other resources—connections, credibility, forum site, staff for forum logistics, or similar support.

Chapter Summary

Chapter 1: Planning the Forum and Obtaining Resources outlined three common types of forums, their goals, benefits, and pitfalls. It then discussed getting your forum plans off the ground—the role of the planning group and sponsors, forum research and design, and developing a timeline and budget. With these basic elements in place, you are ready to roll up your sleeves and start planning the details of the forum.

The next chapter will help you prepare for the big event, including developing an agenda, deciding when and where to hold the forum, promoting and publicizing the forum, and laying the groundwork for evaluating its impact.

Forums on a Shoestring

If you are short on time or money, but still want to convene a forum, here are hints for how you can manage the tasks listed in Chapter 1 with efficiency and style:

- Don't hurry through goal setting. Getting crystal clear on your forum goals is the single-most important step to help ensure that you meet those goals.

- Use a streamlined planning process (see the sidebar, pages 10–11). Keep your design simple—one or two activities or events.

- Have one thoughtful, articulate person who is a good writer draft a short concept paper. Provide opportunities for input from the planning committee and other stakeholders. Avoid the tendency to write by committee.

- Invite people to attend the forum through a letter from a respected leader.

- Get in-kind contributions of food, beverages, space, and printing from local businesses and organizations that would value a little visibility and affiliation with the forum goals.

Preparing for the Forum

You have identified forum goals, created a general design, developed a concept paper, and lined up partners and resources. Now is the time to organize a forum that achieves the desired goals, brings in the number of desired participants, is well coordinated, and keeps within the budget. Ideally, it will also result in even greater payoff—engaged citizens, increased social capital, strengthened community understanding of issues, and high-impact policies.

This chapter discusses five essential tasks necessary for success—to make the forum "not just another forum":

- Create the forum agenda
- Identify resource people
- Handle logistics
- Develop publicity and promotions
- Plan to evaluate the forum

Create the Forum Agenda

Agenda development requires both skill and art. A good agenda is based on the overall forum design. An agenda always starts with a clear understanding of participant expectations and the desired results, balanced against the time available, material to be covered, and space constraints. If the audience is small, you may want to conduct a pre-forum survey to determine what is of most value to the participants. Artistry is required in finding the right balance of product and process—covering the topics thoroughly enough to achieve the forum goals while allowing enough time for participants to interact with each other and the information presented.

Agendas can rapidly become crammed with elements irrelevant to the forum goals. For example, at the outset long lists of people may be given a chance to "say a few words" at the podium: the chair of the planning committee, the presidents of sponsoring organizations, a public official, a neighborhood representative. Then someone introduces the keynote speaker, who talks for a half hour or more. A reaction panel responds to the keynote. Meanwhile, the audience has not yet had a chance to respond to or interact with the information presented.

Resist the temptation to build an agenda where participants listen passively to speakers. People learn more when actively engaged in a process of discovery.

Resist the temptation to build this kind of agenda. Get your audience involved early in the forum. People learn more when information is presented in ways that allow them to actively engage in a process of discovery rather than listening passively. For example, planners of a forum on affordable housing might distribute place-mats with a map of the city and challenge participants to locate affordable housing sites within the city. Discussion questions could then give participants a way to get immediately involved with the forum topic and with each other.

Decisions that need to be made when establishing an agenda include the following:

- Starting, ending, and break times.
- Topics to be covered, sequence, and the amount of time for each.
- Format of presentation (speech, interactive workshop, panel discussion, and so forth). See Appendix C, pages 104–105, for forum design options.
- Level of presentation (beginners require broad, introductory information while experts will be more interested in detailed, industry-specific information).
- Ways information will be presented (written, audiovisual, spoken).
- Process—length of time allowed for question-and-answer sessions, amount of time for movement of audience into small breakout groups, and so forth.

A sample agenda can be found in the sidebar Sample Agenda from a Policy Change Forum in Chapter 4, page 60. Be sure your agenda incorporates the following hints on timing, variety, and speakers.

Timing: Assume you will start five to ten minutes late. Break up the time with brief stretch or coffee breaks every one-and-a-half or two hours. Schedule time for networking and socializing (especially important for community engagement forums). Give agenda items extra time (usually double) if you plan on using language interpreters or signing for speeches. Plan to end on time or early.

Variety: Schedule a mix of general sessions, workshops, audiovisual programs, panels, and roundtables throughout the time. Provide a variety of large and small group experiences, and schedule a reporting-out process for group brainstorming sessions.

Speakers: If you have to schedule speakers immediately after a meal, make sure they are dynamic. Get recommendations—and then get references from people who have heard this person speak in a similar setting.

Characteristics of Adult Learning

When planning the agenda, keep in mind five key characteristics of adult learning:

1. Adults are motivated to learn and goal-oriented.
2. Adults are self-directed learners—they like to engage in a process of mutual inquiry rather than be supplied with facts.
3. Adults learn by doing.
4. Adults learn what is relevant to their current needs.
5. Adults learn best through a variety of methods.

The planning group now has a forum design and agenda. The next challenge is to reach and contract with people who will make the forum sizzle. The following section reviews the many roles that people can play in the forum and gives you ideas on where to find excellent speakers.

Identify Resource People

The term "speaker" in this section refers to a range of resource people who have distinctive skills and qualities and who are able to fill at least one of the roles and responsibilities described on the following pages. Ideally, you will identify and secure speakers as soon as the forum design and agenda have been established. Often the planning group is of vital assistance here. Members can recommend resources based on personal knowledge of the speaker's presentation style and skills, and they can provide the connections and influence to contact and secure the speaker. Identifying resource people can make all the difference between success and failure for the forum. A description of speakers and their roles follows.

Keynote speaker—sets the entire tone for the forum and presents material to frame future discussions. The best keynote speakers are well known in their field, have experience in public speaking and an engaging personality, and can stir an audience to action or reflection.

Moderator—keeps the forum flowing and on schedule. The best moderators are comfortable in front of a large audience, can think quickly on their feet, are a public figure or well known in their field or the community, and know how to handle difficult participants and speakers who talk too long.

Panelists—offer unique points of view and present counterpoint opinions, thus inspiring a rich discussion among the forum participants or initiating a brainstorming session.

Workshop presenters—give credibility to the forum and the information presented in the workshop—especially if they are respected practitioners or experts in their field. The best presenters are effective teachers and speak from a great deal of experience or a specific knowledge base.

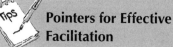

Pointers for Effective Facilitation

- Set a relaxed and open tone.
- Remain objective and neutral.
- Appoint a recorder, reporter, and timekeeper as needed.
- Monitor the process and assist the dialogue rather than actively participating.
- Focus and clarify points made, and summarize key points in the discussion.
- Make sure the group considers a wide range of views.
- Create opportunities for everyone to participate.

Discussion facilitators—conduct large or small group discussions. They can be experienced facilitators or volunteers who attend a short training session prior to the forum. (See the sidebar Pointers for Effective Facilitation. See also the Sample Breakout Group Facilitator Training in Appendix A, pages 72–73.)

Welcomers and closers—contribute to the credibility of the forum and are usually people respected by the audience. A good welcomer will introduce the goals and importance of the forum and create a welcoming atmosphere. A good closer will summarize key points made during the forum, motivate the audience for follow-up action if appropriate, and remind people to fill out evaluation forms. The role of the welcomer or closer is a good opportunity to involve an influential supporter and use their prominence in the community to advance forum goals.

Interpreters—are vital if many people in the audience have language, vision, or hearing challenges. Be sure to include the cost of interpreters in the budget and allow extra time in the agenda for the interpretation (usually double the normal amount of time).

Participants—are also resources for the forum because they are rich in experience and stories and can learn a lot from each other. Build in plenty of time for meaningful dialogue among participants, using structured exercises and work sessions.

How to find resource people

People who can fill the roles and responsibilities described above can be found in surprising places. Here are a few examples, but don't be limited in your search.

- Coworkers and personal contacts
- City, county, state, and federal officials or department heads (library, police, senator, mayor's office)
- Speakers' bureaus of colleges and universities
- Service organizations (YMCA, Jewish Community Centers, Rotary, Junior Leagues, League of Women Voters, American Association of University Women)
- Content experts in healthcare, media, finance, law, community development, or other forum-related discipline
- Chambers of commerce
- Community and business leaders
- Authors
- Participants at other workshops, seminars, and conferences

Contracting with speakers or other resource people

Forum disaster may occur when a speaker fails to show up on time or addresses the wrong topic. At the very least, such a situation can embarrass both the

---

Sample Discussion Ground Rules*

- Everyone gets a fair hearing.
- Seek first to understand, then to be understood.
- Share "air time."
- If you are offended, say so and say why.
- You can disagree, but don't personalize it. Stick to the issue. No name-calling or stereotyping.
- One person speaks at a time.
- What is said in the group stays in the group, unless everyone agrees to change that.

*Adapted from *Smart Talk for Growing Communities* (Pomfret, CT: Topsfield Foundation, 1998) 3.

speaker and forum planners. Make sure that terms are clear with speakers, ideally in a written agreement. Every keynote speaker agreement should contain the following elements:

- The date, time, and location of the forum
- A description of the topic, specific points to be covered, the desired length of the speech, and the amount and type of audience participation desired
- The number and kind of handout materials the speaker will provide and when the materials are needed
- A request for the speaker's biography and a date when it is needed
- The speaker's fee (including travel, lodging, and other expenses if the speaker is not local) and payment terms
- The number of expected participants and their level of understanding of the topic
- A description of the room setup
- Required audiovisual equipment

Agreements with other resource people such as panelists, moderators, and small group facilitators, whether paid or volunteer, should also be written to make sure expectations are clearly defined. Again, if these resource people are not local, clarify who will pay for travel, lodging, food, and other expenses and be sure these costs are reflected in the forum budget.

Additional provisions may be necessary depending on the particular needs of the forum. Other areas to consider are these:

- Expectations for attending meetings or training sessions prior to the forum
- Right to publish a speaker's comments and handout materials; and perhaps an exclusive-use-of-material clause in case the speaker is hired to develop materials for the forum
- A hold-harmless-and-indemnification clause that protects the forum sponsors against liability resulting from the speaker's comments (such a clause might be used in case of a controversial topic)

Securing the speakers you want and setting the forum date is a balancing act. You will have dates in mind before you contact speakers, but sometimes you will end up changing the date based on the availability of your preferred speakers or forum sites.

Handle Logistics

The date, time, facility, and location for the forum are key decisions to make early in the planning and can greatly influence visibility, attendance, and overall impact. Once you have developed a good understanding of the forum design and audience, you can identify a date and time that will work for the majority of people involved. There are several key factors to consider.

Date

Date conflicts can have a big impact on attendance and forum outcomes. Survey other organizations with similar missions—they might be planning a forum for the week before your forum. The planning group can be helpful here if members have wide connections in the community.

Be aware of dates that impact large groups of people—check school calendars for vacation dates and confirm dates for religious holidays for a broad range of faiths. For example, if you are trying to reach the Hmong community, don't set the date on a Hmong religious holiday; or, if the purpose is to influence school district policy, don't set the date on a district-wide testing day. Also verify community celebration dates or unofficial observances such as the "fishing-opener" weekend.

Time

The best time of day to hold a forum depends on the makeup of the target audience. If audience members are businesspeople, hold the forum during the day when they are most likely to attend; if volunteers or citizens would be most interested, hold the forum in the evening or on a weekend. The length of the forum also depends on the forum design and purpose. If the purpose is to hold an educational forum, good learning principles say that three to four hours would have the maximum impact. If the purpose is to engage the participants in a working session, a day or two would allow time for building relationships and getting significant work done.

Time of year may also be a factor in selecting a date and time. For example, what time of year would be best for bringing in a large number of teachers?

Facility

Would business leaders be more likely to show up at a downtown site, in the suburbs, or in a community center for a lunch forum? Would a forum in a government agency meeting room be uncomfortable or unacceptable for the group you are trying to gather to discuss immigration issues? Before considering any facility, know the design and purpose of the forum, the desired date of the forum, the budget for site expenses, and the number of participants expected.

Also be sensitive to the unique needs and expectations of the target audience. For example, consider whether child care is needed. If so, how does this affect the choice of facility? Are there seasonal considerations? Will there be outdoor activities? The answers to these questions will provide the criteria for selecting a forum site.

Types of facilities to consider include

- Convention or retreat centers
- University or college campuses
- Hotels
- Schools
- Business or large nonprofit meeting rooms
- Places of worship
- Special public facilities like museums, zoos, arboretums

Once you have narrowed the list of possible facilities, call the facility for date and time availability. You will also want to visit the facility before finalizing a choice and signing an agreement. Be sure the signed agreement spells out the date, time, costs, constraints, and expectations. Also consider insurance needs. A one-night insurance policy or a rider on an existing policy can cost more than you expect. Usually the facility will have a building coordinator or agent who can help you think through basic decisions such as

- **Room size and setup.** Can the space accommodate the forum design and the number of participants expected? Does the forum design require auditorium-style seating or seating around tables? Will small breakout rooms be needed or simply a large meeting room?
- **Fees.** What are the room rental fees, security fees, building maintenance or janitorial services fees, parking fees, and audiovisual equipment rental fees?

- **Audiovisual equipment.** What equipment is available? Are there any use restrictions? What lighting and sound arrangements will be necessary?

- **Food service.** Does the facility have its own food service? What is the menu? Can a caterer be used instead? Is there space for informal food preparation and service? Can the food service handle dietary or cultural requirements of participants?

- **Parking and transportation access.** How much parking is available and where? Is it handicap accessible? Is the facility on a bus line?

The essential ingredients of your forum are lining up. Of course, to have a forum you also need to have your target audience in attendance. The next section suggests ways to connect with your audience, including media coverage, and how to attract participants through an effective publicity and promotional campaign.

Use Worksheet 5: Forum Site Planning, page 92, as you begin to look for forum sites.

Develop Publicity and Promotions

Begin planning the publicity and any direct mailings at the earliest forum planning stages. A good publicity plan will help you reach the target audience, boost attendance, ensure that the forum will have impact and, as an added bonus, educate the public about the organizations that are planning and sponsoring the forum. The amount and form of the publicity and promotions depend on the purpose of the forum and the target audience. Keep in mind that a successful publicity and promotions campaign for a large public forum will take a minimum of six months.

Know your audience members and the best ways to reach them

Knowing the needs and habits of your target audience is a vital first step; a publicity plan cannot be organized without knowing the audiences you want to reach. You might be developing the most exciting forum in the community, but if people don't know about it or find out too late, it will be poorly attended. It is also possible to spend time and money on useless publicity and promotion. For example, an educational forum for community organizers will not need extensive media coverage but might benefit from meetings with community organizations and a brochure or flyer targeted to community organizers.

Gary Stern, author of *Marketing Workbook for Nonprofit Organizations,* writes, "Gear the materials and techniques to the audience. Think about how your target audience lives and works, where they go, what they are most likely to look at, listen to, or read, who they respect and pay attention to. Then think about what promotion tools fit into that picture."

Stern also says, "Pick the right mix of techniques—within the budget. Don't put all your eggs in one basket. You may have your publics targeted with extreme precision, but even within a narrow group, people have different learning styles and respond best to different approaches. Repeat your message frequently over an extended period of time. This goes along with picking the right mix of tools."[2]

Tools to promote forums

As Stern suggests, promote the forum in a variety of formats and venues. You may want to use some or all of the following tools:

- Direct mail, including brochures, letters, and postcards
- E-mail, listserv, or broadcast fax
- Personalized letters and networking, word of mouth
- Newsletters or newspapers: calendar listings, editorials, news articles, and feature stories in dailies and weeklies
- Posters and flyers
- Presentations and speaking engagements
- Public service announcements on television or radio
- Web site
- Meetings with key constituents

Be sure to communicate the following basics (and triple-check for accuracy!) in any of the tools you choose to use:

- Forum date, time, and location, including correct address and parking instructions and restrictions.
- The "saleable" reasons why people should come, such as a well-known keynote speaker, a chance to learn, a chance to meet people, and the opportunity to get involved.

---

[2] Gary J. Stern, *Marketing Workbook for Nonprofit Organizations Volume I: Develop the Plan* (Saint Paul, MN: Amherst H. Wilder Foundation, 2001) 108-109.

- Whether or not advance registration is required. If it is, be sure the registration process and the form are clear.
- Name, phone number, fax number, and e-mail address of the forum contact.
- Fees charged, if any.

Indicate whether food and child care are provided and whether the site is handicap accessible. Many organizations will want to include information about their organization or mission so that the publicity also serves as an educational tool for the public.

Direct mail

Direct mail allows you to target the promotion to the people most interested in the forum. Direct mail is expensive, so maximize the impact of the mailing. Use an accurate, targeted database and an enticing, clearly worded direct mail offer.

The database is the foundation for a direct mail campaign. It can be built by soliciting lists from forum planning group members, forum sponsors, or other organizations that support the forum goals. You can also rent mailing lists directly from organizations that serve your target audiences or from a "list broker." Information on lists and list brokers can be found in your local library. To avoid wasting resources on duplicate addresses, be sure to collate and eliminate duplicate entries before mailing. If you decide to rent a list, be sure it will reach the people who are interested in your topic. For example, if you are holding a workshop on environmental hazards in the Great Lakes area, you might want to rent the subscriber list of the *Michigan Natural Resources* magazine. E-mails or listservs are also options for reaching large numbers of people, but obtaining accurate addresses presents the same challenges as in direct mail.

Brochures are expensive to produce but can be a good way to attract the target audience's attention and give a professional look to the forum. Be sure the forum brochure contains all the basic written information listed above and visually reflects the focus of the forum—a brochure for a forum on neighborhood block nursing might show nurses with their patients; affordable housing might have hammers and saws; community organizing might have photos of the community activities, and so forth. Brochures should be in the hands of your audience four to six weeks before the forum. If you will be using a graphic artist and an outside printer, remember that those people need time to do their work;

allow up to two months for designing and printing. Some hints for working with printers that can save you money include the following:

- Get quotes from at least three printers (try to support local businesses, but it might be cheaper to ask outside the local area).

- Estimate carefully, and always order more than your first estimate. Setting up the press for a second printing is expensive.

- Delegate the oversight to one or two planning group members who work directly with the designer and seek approval (if needed) from the entire group. It's expensive to bring a designer before the entire planning team and unproductive to frustrate him or her with a variety of conflicting opinions.

- Using one or two colors, standard-size paper, and the printer's "stock" paper for the brochure can save you money.

Sample brochures can be found in Appendix A, pages 78–79.

Media coverage

You may be able to get free media publicity for a large public forum, but it takes a lot of work and planning. The key is to be imaginative. Pay attention to these tips:

- Develop a brief, accurate news release that has a compelling message.

- Keep the news release short (250 to 300 words) but answer most questions someone might ask about the forum. Write a release that intrigues an editor enough to want to publicize the forum.

- Know and meet the deadlines for news releases.

- Keep a press list of your media contacts and a clipping file of all media coverage and update it regularly.

- Get to know people in the media. Send thank-you notes to reporters and editors who publicize your forum, especially if you want to continue the relationship in the future.

- Consider asking a planning group member or sponsor to write an opinion piece or letter to the editor featuring the forum or the topic of the forum.

Public service announcements can reach a wide audience and are free but require a considerable investment in time and planning to pull off. Work with your media contacts for best results. Depending on the forum goals and the target audience, it may also be worth the investment to purchase ads in community or metropolitan newspapers or on the radio.

Any points you make to the public about the forum topics must be grounded in accurate information. Prepare clearly written summaries of information gathered as part of the research early in the forum planning. These summaries can be distributed at the forum, in public announcements, or as part of promotional materials.

The final planning step is deciding how you want to evaluate the forum.

Plan to Evaluate the Forum

The purpose of evaluation is to let you know whether the forum achieved the established goals. Evaluation results can also help in planning future forums. For example, the Wilder Foundation was involved in a forum series titled "Cities at Work." Evaluation of that series showed that 86 percent of participants discussed the topics with someone else, mainly with work colleagues, after the forum. And 56 percent reported joining with others to take action in their communities. Wilder also learned that one of the weakest links in the forum design was the varying skill of small group facilitators, suggesting the need for greater emphasis on facilitator training for future forums. It also learned through a "post-mortem" discussion with the planning committee that follow-up action was confusing to people, suggesting a need to get a clear follow-up plan in place before the forum.

While evaluations can take many shapes and formats, the following may be most useful:

Written feedback forms should be as short as possible (two pages maximum), easy to understand, and easy to tabulate. Provide a variety of response methods; for example, include a rating scale, one to two open-ended questions, and a few multiple-choice questions. Feedback forms work well for a large audience if you have staff who can tabulate the responses or if the form can be scanned into a computer-tabulated program.

Process: Include a written form in every forum packet and schedule a time in the agenda for participants to fill it out. Be sure to place an easily identifiable box or container in a location where people exit the forum to collect the completed evaluations. It's a nice touch to have someone standing by the container encouraging people to place their completed evaluation in the box and thanking them for attending the forum. Sample evaluation forms can be found in Appendix A, pages 74–77.

Follow-up interviews are more expensive to conduct but result in rich, detailed data and can measure long-term retention, behavior changes, or actual follow-up action (vital information when evaluating a community engagement or community action forum).

Process: Interviews (usually by phone) are best conducted by an independent research firm; contract with the firm early.

Pre- and post-test surveys are excellent for measuring quantitatively how much change in knowledge or opinion has occurred as a result of the forum.

Process: This type of evaluation often requires the services of an independent research firm; contract with the firm early and obtain advice regarding the benefits of this method and how it fits with the forum design.

Forum debriefing or retrospective can be beneficial for the planning group, especially if additional forums are planned for the future. A retrospective can provide insight on various aspects of the forum design and planning process, and strengthen teamwork for the future. If done in the spirit of continuous learning, a retrospective can ease the burden of preparing for the next forum and make the next one better than the last.

Process: A facilitator or consultant from outside the planning group may make this a more valuable exercise for the group. The length of the retrospective will vary depending on the number of forums being reviewed, but expect to devote at least a couple hours to the process. Questions to address include the following:

- What did we learn?
- What worked well?
- What could have been improved?
- What follow-up tasks need attention?

- Are there new developments in the community that could affect our follow-up efforts?

- Are there additional opportunities for action that we might tackle to continue to have impact on this issue?

Chapter Summary

Your planning group has identified goals and developed an overall design and agenda for the forum. You have lined up partners and resources and begun to marshal community interest and support through their personal and organizational contacts. You have a date, a site, resource people, and an evaluation plan. The word is getting out in the community, and you are beginning to get response to your publicity and communications efforts.

Now it's time to nail down the nuts and bolts of putting on a forum. Chapter 3: Orchestrating the Event will help you manage the myriad of details involved in putting together a successful forum.

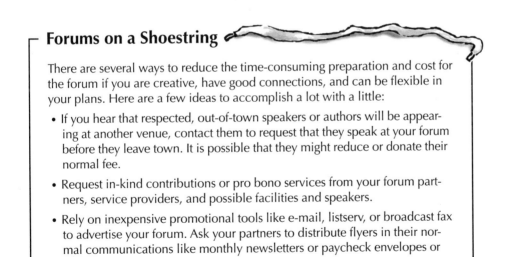

Forums on a Shoestring

There are several ways to reduce the time-consuming preparation and cost for the forum if you are creative, have good connections, and can be flexible in your plans. Here are a few ideas to accomplish a lot with a little:

- If you hear that respected, out-of-town speakers or authors will be appearing at another venue, contact them to request that they speak at your forum before they leave town. It is possible that they might reduce or donate their normal fee.

- Request in-kind contributions or pro bono services from your forum partners, service providers, and possible facilities and speakers.

- Rely on inexpensive promotional tools like e-mail, listserv, or broadcast fax to advertise your forum. Ask your partners to distribute flyers in their normal communications like monthly newsletters or paycheck envelopes or place flyers on countertops.

Orchestrating the Event

You have made the major decisions for the forum, including goals, design, agenda, resource people, dates and times, and promotional methods. These steps establish a solid foundation for a memorable forum. However, the way the event is orchestrated—its style and attention to detail—will make the difference between an adequate forum and a smashing success.

Some of the most frequent complaints from forum participants have to do with the details of forum coordination and administration. The most mundane details are the very things the participants will remember about the forum—especially if something goes wrong: the sound system doesn't work, the room is too cold, the brochure has the wrong date or place on it, parking was terrible.... This chapter will cover the nuts and bolts of forum management. Careful attention to the following four areas will help you achieve the forum goals and avoid major problems:

- Forum coordinator
- Registration
- Facility and food
- Troubleshooting

This chapter is only an overview of the most important elements of event management. For more resources, see Appendix C, which lists books and articles on event management. Also refer to the Forum Checklist, page 106.

Forum Coordinator

An orchestra wouldn't put on a concert without a conductor. Likewise, no one should try to organize a forum without a forum coordinator. The forum coordinator is the primary "go-to" person who is charged with orchestrating all the details—making sure that deadlines are met, work is delegated, and everybody involved gets support and encouragement. The coordinator can be a volunteer or paid staff person, but he or she must be able to devote energy and time and demonstrate commitment to the forum. Small, simple forums may require only one hundred to two hundred hours of prep time. A large, complex forum may require a part- or full-time coordinator for three to twelve months.

The forum coordinator has three main responsibilities:

1. To work closely with the planning group to ensure that implementation steps are in line with the forum design and goals.

2. To implement forum plans within the budget and timeline, coordinating the work of volunteers and staff.

3. To help build planning group and community ownership and interest in the forum through effective and creative communications and encouragement for volunteers and staff.

The forum "office"

It is absolutely essential to keep all forum-related materials in one place. Many successful coordinators prepare a large three-ring binder with tabs or a file drawer with folders to keep all those important phone numbers and addresses, meeting minutes, expense records, and masters for handout packet materials. Other key information that the coordinator will need includes forum goals, sponsors, fact sheets on the sponsoring organizations, budget, timeline, speaker and facility contracts, forum brochures, and price quotes from printers and graphic artists. Having all this information organized in an accessible location saves time looking for lost items and numbers. Well-organized records also facilitate preparation of the next forum.

Volunteer management

Besides maintaining records, the coordinator must manage volunteers. Volunteers devote significant time to the forum's success and may be the primary forum workforce. They include planning group members, representatives from sponsoring organizations, and other community volunteers. They may volunteer to work on a committee, help out at the forum, or be part of the follow-up activities. Therefore, the forum coordinator will need to be clear on what kind of job each volunteer has and what kind of support each volunteer needs to be successful, including training or information required for the job. Volunteers like to be communicated with regularly and recognized for their contributions.

The forum coordinator is the glue for the forum, the person who pulls together all the planning and preparation into a cohesive, effective event. This person will be managing the first critical personal contacts with your target audience through the registration process. The coordinator's style and effectiveness will set the tone for the event.

Registration

Registration is an introduction to the forum and the first point of contact for the participants. A smooth, professional registration process and welcoming sign-in area give a positive first impression and set the tone for the forum. You may want participants to register in advance or at the door, or both, depending on the forum design, fees, budget, and target audience. For example, at-the-door registration may be best for a large public forum on women's health, and the facility, food, and promotion have been donated. For a more specialized forum for healthcare workers for which meeting space is limited, advance registration may be required.

A smooth, professional registration process and welcoming sign-in area give a positive first impression and set the tone for the forum.

Advance registration

Advance registration is expensive in terms of staff time required to manage the process, but it has the advantage of letting you know how many people to expect and how much additional publicity might be needed. If a fee to attend the forum is charged, advance registration can bring in funds with which to start paying expenses.

The registration process must be simple and staff must be prepared to receive and record registrations efficiently. This means that all promotional materials must be explicit about the need for advance registration and contain "reader friendly" registration forms that have clear directions on how to register. For example, if your target audience is primarily Spanish speaking, you might consider having promotional materials printed in both Spanish and English and asking a staff person who is fluent in Spanish to answer participant phone calls and questions.

Inevitably, there will be people who want to attend who have not preregistered, so make sure there is a separate table and extra handouts for walk-in registration.

Incentives for registration may be needed if advance registration is required. Strategies that encourage people to sign up early include offering a break on the registration fee, making early registrants eligible for raffles and drawings, enticing participants with interesting and unusual agenda activities, or offering a free meal to those who register in advance.

Mailing out reminder postcards to those who are registered is a good idea. The postcards can confirm the date, time, and location of the forum and provide any additional information like directions to the facility or parking. Establishing a master database of all registrations and their status (paid, unpaid, sector affiliation, address, and phone) will facilitate this process.

On-site registration

Be clear about what you want from on-site registration. You may want to get each participant's name, organization or affiliation, and where they heard about the forum. This information will be useful if you want to contact participants after the forum. In addition, you may want to collect a registration fee; distribute the handout packet and a blank nametag; or give attendees instructions on where to go and what to do. These considerations will determine the extent of the sign-in process and what kind of staffing is needed at registration.

The registration process must, as much as possible, be streamlined. No participant should have to wait more than ten minutes to register. If the expected audience will be large (more than fifty people), set up several tables for registration. All tables need adequate lighting, a large supply of pens and markers, trash cans for loose paper, and a handout packet for each person attending the forum.

The registration process is a good place to use volunteers if the coordinator provides a short training session ahead of time. Ensure that at least one person is available who can float or deal with unexpected registration issues. If there is a fee to attend, have one person responsible for the cash at all times.

Handout packet

Forum handout packets contribute to the tone you are trying to set for the forum. The packets are part of what welcomes the participants and should include all the necessary information, presented in an attractive and useable way. What and how many handouts to include will depend on the forum's purpose, design, and size. Try to be aware of any special needs participants may have—perhaps handouts printed in other languages or in braille. Consider using paper folders with pockets. The folders can be customized with the name of the forum and sponsoring organizations on the front. Basic packet materials include the following:

- Agenda
- Nametag, if not handed out at the registration table[3]
- A map of the facility including location of breakout rooms, elevators, bathrooms, and phones
- Roster of participants
- Speaker handouts and bios
- Supplementary booklets or workbooks
- Bibliography of reference materials
- Notepaper
- Evaluation form
- Other possible items include child care information and a commitment form (see Chapter 4: Sustaining the Results)

The registration process and handout materials are the introductory pieces to the forum. Now the participants are ready to begin the forum experience itself. A room setup and food arrangement that works well with the forum design, as described below, can greatly enhance that experience for participants.

Facility and Food

In planning the agenda and choosing the facility, the planning group has already established the basic decisions on facility arrangements including the starting and ending times, the budget, the room size and setup, and the type of audio-visual equipment needed. The forum coordinator uses this information and works with the facility to finalize details. Find out who is going to be the facility

---

[3] Nametags serve many purposes. They facilitate participant networking, identify forum organizers and speakers, or indicate small breakout group assignments.

contact for the time of the forum and keep in touch with that person during the planning to prevent mix-ups and communication problems. Before the forum provide the facility with a room setup chart, a detailed agenda with times, and a contact name and number.

Room setup

Details that you will want to work out with the facility before the forum include the following:

- Number and types of seating, such as auditorium style or tables with chairs arranged in different configurations. Be sure to ask for extra tables and chairs and plan preferential seating areas for people who have special needs.

- Speaker needs, such as a podium, a raised platform, or panel discussion tables.

- Kind and location of audiovisual equipment (standing or lapel microphones, overhead or video projector, computer screens, easels or whiteboards, audience microphones, music).

- Location and size of breakout rooms and best ways for the audience to reach them.

- Sight-line problems like pillars, raised stage, people with backs to speaker, or sun glare on audiovisual screens.

- Room acoustics—high ceilings, glass, and hard surfaces can produce an incredible din; carpeting or draperies absorb sound.

- Incidentals like pitchers of water and drinking glasses for speakers, keys for locked doors, or walkie-talkies to contact facility staff if needed.

You must make arrangements with the facility to accommodate people with handicaps. For example, ask the facility whether telephones are equipped with Teletypewriters (TTY) or assistive listening devices for people who are deaf or have speech difficulties. Also ask if there is an area for guide dog relief.

Consider other audience needs. For example, people with certain religious restrictions may require private space for devotions or special food preparation.

Signage

Post signs with the title of the forum in easy-to-spot locations to help participants find the forum site quickly and move through the registration process smoothly. Some facilities will provide a directory at the entrance with the name of the organization, forum name, date, time, and room. There should be signs to indicate the location of restrooms and handicap entrances. Other signs might alert participants to facility rules such as no smoking, off-limit areas to visitors, or no photography. If you decide the forum facility should be decorated to enhance a forum theme, the registration area should carry the "look" as well.

Food and beverages

Food and beverage breaks are an absolute necessity. They provide time for networking and relaxing, break up the day, and reenergize participants. Again, in planning the agenda, you have already set some of the parameters including the number and timing of snacks and meals, the budget, and the target audience. The forum coordinator will work with these parameters to decide who will provide the food (the facility, the participants, a caterer, the planning group) and a menu that can enhance the forum. For example, if the forum is intended to appeal to a multicultural audience, choose a caterer or restaurant that can provide a selection of ethnic foods.

If you use a caterer, be sure the caterer is available on the forum date, has an excellent reputation, and fits within the budget and forum goals. If an ancillary goal is to support and promote local businesses, select a few local restaurants or individual caterers to provide food for the forum. The type of food and food service also depends on the size of the audience and available space for serving and eating. For example, soup is not recommended for groups over fifty (difficult to keep it hot); buffets can work well if set up correctly, but a single buffet line for three hundred people can add an hour to the serving time. A good caterer can help sort through these options and potential barriers.

The forum coordinator has arranged every detail of the room setup and refreshments. You have worked hard to plan a forum that will achieve the goals you set for it. Now is the time to reflect a bit and possibly troubleshoot.

Troubleshooting

An organized, resourceful forum coordinator is key to the management and success of your forum. Despite careful plans and a skilled coordinator, not everything that happens at the forum will be planned. Extra volunteers, quick thinking, and resourcefulness can handle most of the challenges that occur.

While you can't anticipate everything, here are some challenges you might face and how you might prevent or resolve them.

Before the event

Funder does not make the grant that was anticipated: Curtail aspects of the forum (or series) or cancel until more funds can be raised.

Strong conflict breaks out among planning committee members, stalling the planning process: Hire a facilitator or recruit additional members to the committee to bring in additional points of view. Resolve conflicts outside of the meeting room if possible. If necessary, refocus the forum.

Brochures have to be reprinted because of a wrong address or an embarrassing photo resulting in a massive cost overrun: It is worth a cost overrun to avoid any potentially embarrassing or damaging publicity for the forum. Approach a funder to explain the overrun and ask for funds to cover it, or approach others for more funding. Try to get donated printing.

The facility requests that you sign a contract and name the facility as an "additional insured" on your insurance policy: Before signing any contract, discuss it with your attorney and insurance professional. Be aware of any unusual hazards and never let your zeal to use a facility color your judgment.

Your computer crashes taking your entire registration list with it: In this case, prevention is your best medicine. Back up your key information nightly and store it in a separate location, or share your list with a forum partner. You should also save any paper registration forms you receive. These could be useful when re-creating a lost registration list.

During the event

Sun glare makes the speaker's overhead presentation unreadable: Test for lighting prior to facility rental. Have handouts on the presentation prepared or promise to mail them to all participants after the forum (and, of course, follow through on the promise).

A participant suddenly experiences severe chest pains: Immediately call the emergency medical number of the area. The moderator should inform participants of the emergency and how it is being addressed and announce a short coffee break or continue with the forum agenda, if possible. A participant may volunteer to help if medically qualified.

Someone in the audience becomes too talkative, angry, or aggressive and begins to disrupt the forum: A skilled moderator can tactfully handle most people. In very difficult cases, announce a coffee break and have a couple of members of the planning group or the moderator take the person aside to discuss the issue less publicly. Be prepared to ask the person to leave the forum (with police assistance if necessary) if no resolution can be achieved.

Speaker talks for one hour but was only allotted a half hour in the agenda: Assign someone in the audience to flash time cards warning the speaker of the time limit. Be prepared to shorten or eliminate another portion of the agenda.

A fire alarm goes off or a tornado is sighted in the vicinity and sirens sound: The map of the facility in the handout packet should be marked with the location of safe areas. The moderator should use the microphone and direct people to leave in an orderly manner.

The audiovisual equipment malfunctions: Try to avoid this by hiring an audiovisual technician or using a knowledgeable volunteer (with demonstrated expertise) to help with the audiovisual equipment. The forum coordinator should bring extra light bulbs and extension cords. If problems occur despite your preparations, be creative: for example, if sound equipment fails, relocate the speaker to the center of the room (rather than the front of the stage), and have the audience move closer to the speaker. If the overhead projector fails, bring out flip charts and designate writers to take notes.

Interpretation (spoken or sign) takes much longer than anticipated: As mentioned earlier, if interpreters are to be used, plan on twice the time for presentations and discussion. Involve interpreters in the planning stages to ensure that realistic timelines are established.

Speaker arrives late or not at all: Confirm key resource people a week prior to the forum. Have the speaker's cell phone or office numbers handy. Have a backup plan ready in case someone doesn't show up.

A vendor hired to help with the event causes an injury to a forum participant and turns out to be uninsured: For example, a forum participant trips over an uninsured photographer's equipment and twists an ankle. Always obtain a certificate of insurance from anyone providing services for the forum. If the service is part of a partner's contribution, draft a "memo of agreement" outlining responsibilities. This will help to avoid assumptions about who is responsible for what aspect of the event.

The numbers of participants who sign up for follow-up task groups far exceed expectations: Be prepared to add sign-up sheets and groups and obtain increased funding to support the interest.

Chapter Summary

You have been thoughtful about the forum design and goals, and all the speakers, volunteers, and staff are ready. The facility is prepared for your arrival and the food is on its way. Now the fun or chaos (or both) really starts! Unexpected requests and situations appear to challenge your ingenuity. But, relax—this is normal and natural. Prior planning will help to avert some crises on the day of the forum but, inevitably, something unexpected will occur. Extra volunteers, quick thinking, and resourcefulness can handle most challenges that occur. The result will be an exciting, energy-filled forum.

Capturing the energy that people feel at the end of a forum and focusing that energy on commitment to action is the next challenge facing you. Chapter 4: Sustaining the Results will help you mobilize people toward positive action and concrete results.

Forums on a Shoestring

There are several ways to minimize the work and expense of coordinating and conducting a forum. If you have very little time and money for a forum, be sure to rely on the following:

- Register guests at the door rather than in advance. This minimizes the staff time and promotional expense involved in advance registration. You will want to have sign-in sheets to capture names of participants for future contact.

- Provide a minimal handout packet (which can be assembled quickly) and blank nametags rather than preprinted ones (but be sure to mail additional information to participants after the forum if requested).

- Provide simple food (cheese and crackers, pieces of fruit, and canned drinks) that doesn't require a great deal of preparation but keeps participants' energy levels up.

Sustaining the Results

The energy and commitment to action that emerge from a successful forum can be captured and transformed into concrete action at individual, organizational, or community-wide levels. However, the plans for this transformation must be made, or at least considered, *before* the forum, ideally as part of the initial forum planning. In some cases, it will take as much energy and staff time to follow up after the forum as it does to hold the event. But sustaining the results—positive change in the community—is the payoff of such preparation.

Understanding the necessary ingredients to bring about change is important for achieving changes after a forum. Michael Beer at Harvard University has developed a simple framework to use in thinking about change.

Change happens when three ingredients are present—dissatisfaction with the present, a vision for how things can be different, and understanding the first step needed to bring about the change.

Beer postulates that change happens when three ingredients are present—dissatisfaction with the present, a vision for how things can be different, and understanding the first step needed to bring about the change. The three of these together must be stronger than the perceived cost of bringing about the change. If any one of these ingredients is missing or too weak, motivations will be weaker than the perceived cost of bringing about change, and change is then unlikely to happen.

For example, if a forum is held to get parents more involved in their children's learning and school activities, there is a greater chance of success if parents are presented with research that demonstrates different achievement levels of children with and without parental involvement, given concrete ways they can be more involved, and challenged to take action immediately after the forum. If parents understand the positive consequences of high parental involvement and know a few practical ways to become involved, they are more likely to be motivated to become active.

In another situation, a forum might do a masterful job of presenting the need for more affordable housing and offer several promising approaches used in other communities. But if the forum doesn't allocate adequate time to discuss strategies for increasing the scale of affordable housing and set some next steps in motion—with public accountability for leadership of these steps—the opportunity for meaningful change in policy or practice is left up to chance.

In order for a forum to bring about lasting, desired changes, all of these factors—dissatisfaction, vision, first steps, and the cost of change—need to be considered when planning the forum, during the forum, and in follow-up efforts.

The kinds of efforts and activities that are needed after a forum will vary depending on the goals of each forum and the needs of the community. Follow-up steps can range from solidifying the learnings acquired by individuals to engaging participants and the broader community in joint efforts to achieve changes in policy or the community.

This chapter suggests ideas to use before, during, and after the forum to increase the likelihood of achieving the desired results.

Before the Forum

Before the forum, clarify what you hope will happen after the forum and begin to make plans for follow-up action. As mentioned in Chapter 1, a forum is usually selected as a strategy to accomplish a specific goal—education, engagement, or action. Plans for follow-up action should reflect that goal. Keep in mind the three necessary ingredients for change—dissatisfaction, vision, and knowing the first step.

Here are suggestions for pre-forum work that can foster follow-up action:

- Make sure the design and agenda of the forum incorporate ways to focus and direct the information, energy, and commitment that will result from a well-designed forum. (See ideas in the During the Forum section on page 56.)

- Hold focus groups or interviews with potential participants or decision makers to build relationships and to better understand their concerns, their levels of understanding of an issue, and their ideas for change and the steps to bring about change. If at all possible, get these people involved in the planning group.

Before the forum, clarify what you hope will happen after the forum and begin to make plans for follow-up action.

- Conduct research or gather information on the topics and develop summaries to hand out at the forum. These summaries can help participants identify reasons for dissatisfaction with the current state of affairs or first steps that can be taken, both critical parts of the change formula.

- Design the forum to include time for participants to connect with each other in-depth, learn about each other's viewpoints, and discover new possibilities for the future. Such interaction helps participants build a vision for change. Resist the temptation to schedule an endless series of talking heads.

- Research and create a list of organizations doing work on the topic. The list can serve as a resource for participants if they are motivated to take action after the forum.

- Recruit sponsors and planning group members to lead post-forum action groups and to host the first post-forum meeting.

- Recruit sponsoring organizations that will donate resources for follow-up action, including meeting space, child care for meeting participants, leadership, or money.

The pre-forum work involves planting seeds and making sure conditions are right for growing the energy and enthusiasm for carrying out forum goals. The next section suggests methods you can use during the forum to encourage participants to commit to follow-up action.

During the Forum

During the forum you have the greatest opportunity to generate enthusiasm and commitment to working toward change. Following are things you can do to increase the potential for follow-up action.

- Provide simple handouts with ideas for how people can become more involved on an issue, including names of organizations or web sites to go to for more information on the forum topic. This method helps participants identify first steps that can be taken after the forum.

- Structure time during the forum for small group discussions. These give people a chance to talk about their experiences and become inspired by other people's ideas. Sometimes, such small groups decide to meet again outside of the forum to have a more in-depth conversation.

- If policy change is a goal, hold a lunch meeting for policy makers and business and community leaders on the day of the public forum to inform them of the forum goals, highlight material to be covered, and ask for their commitment to support the community's work on the issue. A meeting can also be held after the forum to report on material presented and strategy ideas that emerged.

- Close the forum with a way that participants can make a commitment to action. Some ideas that encourage commitment and follow-through are

  The buddy system: Participants set a date for a phone call to a fellow forum participant to check in and discuss progress on the agreed-upon action.

  Postcard: Participants address a postcard to themselves stating what action they will be taking after the forum. This technique gives participants permission to confidentially take action that is comfortable for them and most appropriate for their personal situation. The postcards are collected at the end of the forum and mailed to participants in three to six months as a reminder of their commitment.

  Action groups: Give participants an opportunity to gather at the forum with others who are passionate about working on an issue. The group may emerge from the forum with an agreement to meet at another time and place to further develop action plans. Or set aside twenty minutes during the forum for the first organizing meeting.

Sponsor commitments: Sponsoring organizations make a public commitment to change their own policies or practices relevant to the forum topic and describe what those changes will be. These commitments will inspire and inform other people to make similar commitments.

Use multiple methods before and during a forum to encourage follow-up action. You will be reinforcing a message—that the forum is about more than one or two days of talk. The forum is part of a larger purpose and longer-term process to accomplish positive change in people's lives, families, and communities.

The next section addresses what you might do to capitalize on the energy generated during the forum and ensure that desired changes do occur.

After the Forum

There are several ways to follow up after a forum, depending on the kind of action or commitment you wish to achieve. Keep in mind your forum goals. If you aim for community education, use methods that will reinforce learning. If you aim for community engagement, provide avenues for people to become engaged quickly and in concrete things. If you aim for community action, quickly disseminate information about action opportunities.

Following are various methods that will support action after your forum.

Forum summaries or formal written reports

Send participants a summary of information presented at the forum, including forum evaluation results or participant feedback, to reinforce learnings from the forum, provide ways to continue relationships made at the forum, and promote the sponsoring organizations. In the same mailing, include a card or memo thanking participants for attending the forum, a copy of a news clipping reporting new information that has emerged since the forum, or a listing about where they can go for more information on the topic. A summary of information is often the major follow-up effort for an educational forum.

A more formal written report of forum results, ranging from a short two-page summary to a twenty-page bound booklet, could go to funders, sponsors, or decision makers. If the forum's goals are community action, make sure that officials, elected delegates, and others in positions of power receive the material as well.

Coordinated community action

Community work is a dynamic process, ill suited to orderly, linear planning models. If you are successful in engaging citizens and building ownership and commitment, people will want to be involved in co-creating the follow-up action process and activities. And people's natural inclinations often make "doing" much easier and more stimulating than "planning." Therefore, a critical aspect of coordinating community action is orchestrating an organic, often messy process. Don't try to control everything. Positive, and sometimes problematic, action will occur outside of the control of the planning group.

The planning group or sponsors supporting post-forum action can provide needed leadership, coordination, and communications. They can also link follow-up efforts with other activities in the community focused on similar issues. Following are specific ideas for encouraging and supporting public action on issues.

1. Make sure that by the end of the forum, participants know about opportunities for action and what roles they can play. Their energy and enthusiasm for getting involved are highest at that moment. Capture and focus that energy into concrete commitments.

2. Allow the structure of follow-up action to evolve. If the community is to fully own the results, it must be part of creating a workable structure or form.

3. Some groups have found that working on small projects first helps to test ideas and build confidence to take on bigger issues.

4. Publicize and celebrate early successes to keep the momentum going.

5. Communicate frequently and broadly. Without regular communication, people easily assume nothing is changing. Remember to use a wide variety of tools—newsletters, e-mails, action alert memos, newspaper articles, action plan documents, and web sites.

6. Be prepared for controversy. When many diverse community leaders work together, controversial issues will arise and resolution can be challenging. If conflict happens, view it positively: it simply indicates that

people care deeply about the issues. Outside facilitation may be needed to help them find common ground.

7. Watch for and support leaders that emerge from the group so that they can progressively assume responsibility for joint action.

Policy change efforts

In the case of a community action forum, the forum is only the launching pad for increased attention or action on an issue or changes in policy. It is often one part of a more lengthy strategy intended to clarify public sentiment and influence policy. Success is measured by whether or not a change in policy actually occurred.

A community action forum can provide three basic elements for effective policy work: a body of information about an issue, community opinions about the issue, and a clearer understanding about what a more desirable policy might be.

Some ways to increase the likelihood of support for policy change include both top-down policy work and bottom-up organizing work, as described here.

• Monitor the legislative, budgeting, or public policy process and identify groups and bills that affect your issues.

• Produce brief, clearly written position papers on the topics you wish to influence, including information generated for or during the forum. Disseminate these to elected officials via personal meetings with forum sponsors or members of the planning group. If you have used outside experts as presenters at the forum, or best-practices ideas from other communities, include summaries of this material.

• Develop clear and concrete statements of recommended policy changes. Be sure to include the names and affiliations of people who were instrumental in creating the recommendations.

Minnesota Decides, a collaboration of six public, private, and nonprofit organizations,[4] is an example of how a deliberate, strategic policy change process can generate significant public support and action on an issue. (See Chapter 1, page 18, for a description of Minnesota Decides as a community action forum.) The program was created in 1997 in response to concerns over youth tobacco

---

[4] Minnesota Decides is a Blue Cross and Blue Shield of Minnesota Foundation community health initiative in conjunction with the Minnesota Department of Health, Minnesota Department of Human Services, Office of the Minnesota Attorney General, Association of Minnesota Counties, and Minnesota Smoke Free Coalition.

use and the growing number of tobacco-related deaths and illnesses in Minnesota. Conceived as a statewide effort to develop and implement a comprehensive community-based set of recommendations, it was built from the grassroots up and refined by participants in a series of forums. Following the forums, state and national experts were asked to comment on recommendations that emerged from the forums and to add their perspectives. As a result, three major action recommendations were developed.

1. A strong and sustained commitment from local and state government and the private sector to reduce tobacco use, including

   - A significant increase in the price of tobacco
   - Creation of a clearinghouse to provide assistance and resources for communities to adopt programs that have proven successful in other communities
   - Financing for school-based programs to reach youth with effective prevention and cessation programs
   - Funding for smoking cessation programs
   - Investment in research on issues ranging from basic science to related social and public policy issues

2. An ongoing public information and education program to inform the public on the health hazards and addictive nature of tobacco, counter the glamorization of tobacco use, and reinforce tobacco abstinence as the norm.

3. An infrastructure to sustain and support tobacco reduction efforts and integrate activities proposed for six community settings.

The partnership prepared briefing materials on tobacco activities in other states. It facilitated the development of community plans in pilot communities, and deployed media relations activities

---

Tips

Sample Agenda from a Policy Change Forum

Minnesota Decides: A Community Blueprint for Tobacco Reduction
Statewide Summit

AGENDA

Day 1

1. Welcome
2. Report from ten community forums
   - Reaction panel
   - Audience discussion
3. Lunch and panel discussion: critical issues in reducing tobacco use in Minnesota
4. Goal-setting session: small groups
5. Work sessions (six goal areas: points of access, worksites, schools and child care, public places, healthcare facilities, families)
6. Dinner and evening program: Advertising: demon or deliverance?

Day 2

1. Welcome and overview
2. Work session reports, discussion, and plan development
3. Lunch and keynote address
4. Continuation of work session reports and plan development
5. Next steps and concluding remarks

to keep communities updated on progress. It also produced and widely distributed a seventy-two-page blueprint for Minnesota tobacco reduction, which described roles for healthcare and managed care organizations to play. Finally, the partnership gathered a large number of stakeholders across the state committed to the issue, creating significant visibility and momentum for the policy goals.

On page 60 is the agenda used in a large, two-day, statewide forum to create a plan and follow-up action steps. Note that the majority of time in the forum is devoted to small group work sessions rather than presentations, and there is time at the end to finalize follow-up action steps.

Chapter Summary

The success of a forum is often measured by whether or not a change actually occurred with individuals or the broader community. Strategies to support follow-up action vary depending on the goals of the forum and the needs of the community. Forum planners can take many steps before, during, and after a forum to sustain the energy and commitment of participants, influence decision makers, and mobilize communities to bring about positive change.

Forums on a Shoestring

Chapter 4: Sustaining the Results discussed how to support post-forum efforts. If you are really on a shoestring, the tendency is to breathe a sigh of relief at the end of the forum and hope that individuals or organizations will be motivated to continue on their own. This "hope-for-the-best" strategy is reasonable if you hold a community education forum and it is a one-time event. If your goal is community engagement or action, you can't rest when the forum is over. Hints to sustain results on a shoestring include these:

- Enlist other groups in the community to take leadership on aspects of follow-up work that fit with their mission.
- Set up a web site where you can post all meeting minutes and action plans, eliminating the need for costly and time-consuming mailings. Or set up a listserv to accomplish the same thing.
- Gather all the evidence you can find that the forum accomplished its intended goals, so that next time you can raise enough money to support doing it with less financial strain.

Conclusion

A community forum is a means to an end, not an end in itself. Forums are held to educate people, engage people in the work of communities, and mobilize public support for policy and action. Forums are part of a larger purpose and longer-term process to accomplish positive change in individual lives, families, and communities.

Remembering these four principles will help you be successful with your forum:

1. Be clear on the ends you want to achieve.

2. Design a forum that will accomplish those ends, with a well-chosen planning group.

3. Pay attention to details. Seamless logistics contribute mightily to a memorable event.

4. Follow through by supporting follow-up action.

This book was written to help you plan and orchestrate a forum or forums to achieve your desired goals. Now you have the inspiration and the tools to create your own successful forum.

Sample Documents

Sample Forum Budget

The following budget represents projected costs and revenues for a one-day forum with two out-of-town speakers, continental breakfast, and box lunches. Estimated attendance for this forum is 250 people. The budget assumes broad direct mail promotion but no advertising costs. It also assumes that sponsors will contribute both financial and in-kind support.

Every forum will have a different configuration of revenue and expense items. Use this sample budget as a guide. Worksheet 2: Forum Budget, page 85, will be of further assistance in developing your own forum budget.

REVENUE		
Grants		**$22,309**
XYZ Corporation	6,000	
Community Foundation	6,000	
Private Foundation	5,809	
Family Foundation	4,500	
Partner Contributions		**6,000**
6 Partners @ $1,000 =	6,000	
In-kind Contributions		**6,305**
Donated admin. support staff =	2,625	
Donated printing =	3,200	
Donated planning meeting food =	480	
Participant Fees		**0***
TOTAL REVENUE		**$34,614**

* Participation fees for this forum are covered by contributions and grants

EXPENSE

Salary/Benefits (Includes benefits @ 25%)		**$6,795**
Forum coordinator: .25 FTE for 4 months =	4,170	
Admin. support: .3 FTE for 3 months =	2,625	
Contractor Fees		9,750
Speakers: 2 @ $1,000/day =	2,000	
Graphic design =	2,800	
Facilitators: 6 @ $75 =	450	
Research =	4,500	
Printing and Copying		3,525
Brochure =	3,200	
Miscellaneous copying: 3,250 copies @ $.10 =	325	
Postage		1,746
Bulk: 5,800 pieces @ $.12 =	696	
First class: 1,500 pieces @ $.50 =	750	
Courier: 20 @ $15 =	300	
Travel for Presenters		1,720
Airfare: 2 trips @ $800 =	1,600	
Taxis: 4 trips @ $30 =	120	
Room/Board for Presenters		1,000
4 days @ $250/day =	1,000	
Program/Office Supplies		400
Miscellaneous =	400	
Food		4,980
Forum food: 250 people @ $18 =	4,500	
Planning meetings: 8 people x 12 meetings @ $5 =	480	
Room/Equipment Rental		1,000
Room rental =	600	
Equipment: 3 mikes; overhead projector =	400	
Subtotal		**$30,916**
Overhead (12%)		**3,698**
TOTAL EXPENSE		**$34,614**

Sample Forum Concept Paper

Housing: A Roof for Everyone

A community forum to stimulate collaborative action to address the urgent need for affordable housing in our community.

Background

If our city and the region grow at the expected rate over the next twenty-five years, we will have to accommodate nine thousand additional households. Three factors contribute to the urgency of this challenge:

1. There is currently a significant scarcity of affordable housing of all kinds in the city.

2. Our traditionally stable neighborhoods, especially in the areas immediately surrounding the downtown area, are experiencing noticeable decline in the quality of the housing stock and other indicators of community health and vitality.

3. The current vacancy rate for rental housing in the city is less than 2 percent.

Our challenges are both immediate and long term. What do we need to do now to ensure that we have affordability, choice, and quality in our housing stock for the future?

For the last three months, eight organizations—a mix of nonprofit, public, and private sector groups—have been meeting to share information and plans regarding the housing crisis. One conclusion we have reached is that many more people and organizations need to be brought into the conversation if we are to make any headway in solving this challenge. Another conclusion is that to address this long-term, complex issue, sustained commitment from many different groups will be required.

Holding a community forum is the first step in calling public attention to the issue and in identifying other individuals and groups who want to be part of a collaborative effort to begin solving the housing crisis.

Goals

A community forum—*Housing: A Roof for Everyone*—will achieve three goals:

1. Build awareness of the nature of the housing crisis and develop an understanding of how demographic and economic trends affect housing production, consumer demand, and availability of affordable housing options in the city.

2. Learn concrete approaches that have worked in other cities to ensure our housing stock will provide a range of affordability and housing choices for our city's residents in the future.

3. Enlist at least fifteen additional nonprofit, public, and private organizations who want to be part of a long-term, collaborative effort to address this issue.

Target audience

1. Concerned residents
2. City, county, and metropolitan policy makers concerned about the affordable housing shortage
3. Neighborhood and community-based housing development organizations
4. Private sector lenders and developers
5. City planning department staff

Pre-forum research

- Demographic trends and projections
- Data on the city's housing stock by neighborhood
- Best practices from other cities regarding affordable housing programs, employer-assisted housing, and housing preservation programs
- Potential speakers and discussion facilitators

Design elements

- Forum should be a full day on a Saturday in April.
- The morning session will include a presentation of research data on trends affecting housing development, breakout group sessions, and a panel presentation on what other cities have done.

- Lunch will be served.
- The afternoon session will include breakout group discussion on the panel presentation and the formation of "action teams" based on interest in themes generated through discussion.
- Closing the forum will include a summary of the forum, a challenge to participants to stay active through their "action team," and a thank-you for participating in the forum.
- Forum follow-up will include a written summary of evaluation results and phone calls to action team members one month after the forum.

Planning group and sponsorship

The eight convening organizations will sponsor the forum. Sponsoring organizations have committed to actively participate in planning and promoting the event, help raise needed funds, contribute $1,000 each (six partners) or in-kind contributions (two partners) to defray expenses, and provide leadership on follow-up efforts.

Staffing

The neighborhood community development corporation will serve as fiscal agent for the forum and will provide a staff person to serve as forum coordinator. The planning group will reimburse the Community Development Corporation for the staffing and other overhead costs it will incur.

Evaluation

Two evaluation methods will be used.

1. Immediate post-forum feedback will be obtained via an e-mail survey of participants. It is estimated that 90 percent of projected participants have access to e-mail, and that e-mail survey response is higher than the average return rate from surveys distributed at the event. This e-mail survey will be conducted within the week following the forum.

2. An independent research group will conduct telephone interviews with a 30 to 50 percent sample of participants approximately three months after the forum to determine what actions, if any, participants or their organizations have undertaken as a result of attendance at the forum.

Cost

A full forum budget is attached. Following is a summary of expected revenue and expense items associated with the forum, including in-kind contributions.

REVENUE		
Grants	$22,309	
Partner contributions	6,000	
In-kind contributions	6,305	
TOTAL REVENUE		**$34,614**

EXPENSE		
Salaries and independent contractors	$16,545	
Printing and copying	3,525	
Food	4,980	
Miscellaneous	5,866	
Overhead	3,698	
TOTAL EXPENSE		**$34,614**

Funding plans

Forum partners and sponsors will contribute over one third of the cost of the forum, either in cash or in-kind contributions. Two thirds of the forum cost will need to be raised from outside sources. Three sources—the XYZ Corporation, the Community Foundation, and a private foundation—will be asked to each contribute one third of the balance of funds required. Each of these three sources has a long and strong commitment to housing in our community.

Sample Breakout Group Facilitator Training

Use this sample breakout group facilitator training as a guide in developing a facilitator training for your forum. This is an example of a two-hour training session held just prior to the event to train facilitators on three major portions: (1) background on the event's goals; (2) overview of the breakout group agenda; and (3) tips and practice in facilitating group discussions.

Background for forum facilitators

The goals of the forum are to begin to create a neighborhood vision and to generate community participation, ownership, and enthusiasm for neighborhood planning. During the forum, breakout groups will be assigned to various discussion topics. Your job will be to facilitate a breakout group discussion and make sure the sponsors have a legible record of your group discussion at the end of the meeting. Following is the agenda for the breakout group discussions and a description of your role in facilitating them.

Breakout group agenda

1. People will move into their breakout groups. Everyone will have a number on their nametag that will correspond to the various groups. (5 minutes)

2. Introductions. (10 minutes)
   - Introduce yourself.
   - Ask people in your group to introduce themselves.
   - Remind people of your group's assignment:
   We will have forty minutes to answer our group's question. Thirty minutes will be spent generating ideas and ten minutes will be spent prioritizing the ideas.

3. Decide who will serve as recorder and reporter.
   - Recorder—legibly record ideas on newsprint sheets.
   - Reporter—report the group's top four ideas to the large group.

4. Brainstorm answers to your group's assigned question. (30 minutes)
   - Not everyone will understand the term "brainstorming." If needed, describe what you are doing as:
     - Generating a lot of different ideas
     - Suspending judgment (all ideas are good and won't be criticized)
     - Valuing contribution (everyone's ideas are important)
   - Come up with a list of ideas. Have the recorder tape the sheets up on the wall and record ideas as people brainstorm.

5. Prioritize the ideas—quickly! (10 minutes)
    - Have everyone pick his or her top five ideas.
    - Count votes by a show of hands for each idea, and mark the number of votes next to each idea.
    - Circle the four ideas with the most votes.

6. Report to the full group: (2–3 minutes for each group)
    - The question you were addressing.
    - Your group's top four ideas.

Hints for facilitating group discussions

1. In general:
    - Relax and have fun! Humor and a relaxed attitude will help the group enjoy the discussion and will generate more and better ideas.
    - Encourage everyone to participate.
    - Watch the time. Ask someone in the group to report the time at ten-minute intervals, and when you have five minutes left.

2. If you can't get the group to begin:
    - Ask everyone to write down two ideas, and then go around the circle twice with everyone contributing one idea at a time.
    - Use humor to loosen the group up. Make fun of yourself, not of the group.

3. If someone dominates the conversation:
    - Thank them for their thoughts and ask if anyone else has other ideas.
    - Ask to hear from those who haven't spoken.
    - Suggest that the person call or write the sponsor after the forum to discuss their ideas in more detail.

4. If the group runs out of ideas:
    - Suggest a new or related topic that hasn't been discussed.
    - Ask someone to say more about an interesting idea that was suggested.
    - Ask if anyone has an idea that was not listed before you start prioritizing.

5. Instructions for recorders:
    - Record ideas legibly.
    - Try to use people's own words as much as possible.

Thank people.

Sample Luncheon Evaluation Form

Cities at Work Forum Series Housing: A Roof for Everyone

Participant Feedback

In order to help us improve the quality of future lunch forums, please complete this feedback form. Your thoughtful comments, criticisms, and ideas are very much appreciated.

1. Please rate the overall value and usefulness of this lunch forum to you:

   Terrible   Poor   OK   Good   Very Good   Fantastic

2. Thinking about today's discussion, what would you like to see done differently in our community?

   _____

   _____

   _____

   _____

   _____

   _____

   _____

   _____

   _____

   _____

   _____

Thanks for taking the time to complete this form.

Sample Forum Evaluation Form

Cities at Work Forum Series Housing: A Roof for Everyone

Participant Feedback

In order to help us improve the quality of future forums, please complete this evaluation form. Your thoughtful comments, criticisms, and ideas are very much appreciated.

Please rate the following aspects of the program:

	Terrible	Poor	OK	Good	Very Good	Fantastic
The quality of the information presented:	1	2	3	4	5	6
The amount of time allowed for audience participation and discussion:	1	2	3	4	5	6
The extent to which you can apply the information presented to your school, work, or community:	1	2	3	4	5	6
The overall value and usefulness of this forum to you:	1	2	3	4	5	6

What are the one or two most important ideas from today's forum?

_____

_____

_____

_____

Are there any topics you would like to see addressed at future forums?

_____

_____

_____

_____

Other comments?

_____

_____

_____

_____

_____

_____

Do you or your organization want to be informed of future affordable
housing efforts?

Contact Name _____

Address (with ZIP code) _____

_____

_____

_____

E-mail & Fax _____

_____

Thanks for taking the time to complete this form.

Sample Forum Participant Follow-up Evaluation Form

Cities at Work Forum Series Housing: A Roof for Everyone

An independent research firm was hired to conduct telephone interviews three months after the forum series with a random sampling of participants to obtain an understanding of the long-term impact of the forum series. Forum participants were interviewed using the following questions to find out to what extent respondents had gained new information or had taken action steps since the forums. If respondents reported that they had, they were asked to describe what they had learned or what they had done. The feedback helped to improve the quality of future forums.

1. Did you participate in any of the Cities at Work forums? Which ones?

2. Why did you decide to participate in one of the forums?

3. Did you gain any new information from participating in the community forums?

4. Have you discussed any of this year's forum topics with anyone since attending the sessions?

5. Since attending the forums have you joined with others in any kind of action in your community?

6. Would you recommend these forums to others? Why or why not?

7. Looking back on the experience, what would you say was most useful? *(multiple-choice range of: presentation, information, breakout groups)*

8. If you could give some advice to the planners of future forums, what would it be?

At this point, the participant was asked to respond to some demographic questions such as gender, location of residence, racial or ethnic background, age, political leanings, highest grade completed, religious orientation, and income. The demographic data was useful in determining if forum goals and target audience were reached and if future forums will require different outreach strategies.

Sample Forum Promotional Brochures

Following are examples of brochures created for the Cities at Work forum series.

Cities at Work 2

A 1997 forum series to promote dialogue and discovery about Saint Paul's future

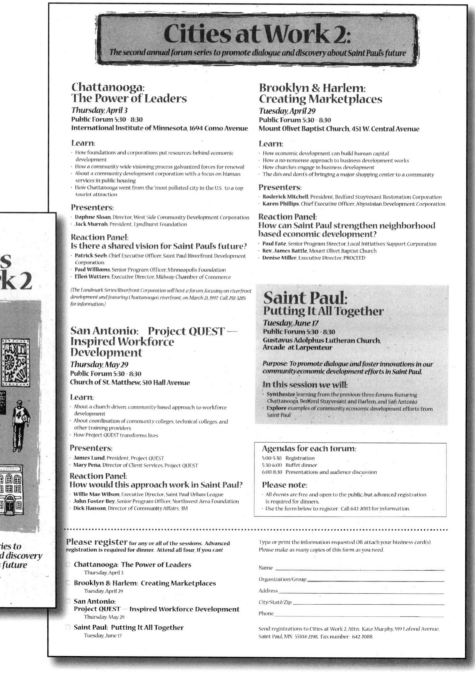

Cities at Work 2:

The second annual forum series to promote dialogue and discovery about Saint Paul's future

Chattanooga: The Power of Leaders

Thursday, April 3
Public Forum 5:30 - 8:30
International Institute of Minnesota, 1694 Como Avenue

Learn:
- How foundations and corporations put resources behind economic development
- How a community-wide visioning process galvanized forces for renewal
- About a community development corporation with a focus on human services in public housing
- How Chattanooga went from the 'most polluted city in the U.S.' to a top tourist attraction

Presenters:
- **Daphne Sloan**, Director, West Side Community Development Corporation
- **Jack Murrah**, President, Lyndhurst Foundation

Reaction Panel:
Is there a shared vision for Saint Paul's future?
- **Patrick Seeb**, Chief Executive Officer, Saint Paul Riverfront Development Corporation
- **Paul Williams**, Senior Program Officer, Minneapolis Foundation
- **Ellen Watters**, Executive Director, Midway Chamber of Commerce

(The Landmark Series/Riverfront Corporation will host a forum, focusing on riverfront development and featuring Chattanooga's riverfront, on March 21, 1997. Call 292-3285 for information.)

San Antonio: Project QUEST — Inspired Workforce Development

Thursday, May 29
Public Forum 5:30 - 8:30
Church of St. Matthew, 510 Hall Avenue

Learn:
- About a church-driven, community-based approach to workforce development
- About coordination of community colleges, technical colleges, and other training providers
- How Project QUEST transforms lives

Presenters:
- **James Lund**, President, Project QUEST
- **Mary Pena**, Director of Client Services, Project QUEST

Reaction Panel:
How would this approach work in Saint Paul?
- **Willie Mae Wilson**, Executive Director, Saint Paul Urban League
- **John Foster Bey**, Senior Program Officer, Northwest Area Foundation
- **Dick Hanson**, Director of Community Affairs, 3M

Brooklyn & Harlem: Creating Marketplaces

Tuesday, April 29
Public Forum 5:30 - 8:30
Mount Olivet Baptist Church, 451 W. Central Avenue

Learn:
- How economic development can build human capital
- How a no-nonsense approach to business development works
- How churches engage in business development
- The do's and don'ts of bringing a major shopping center to a community

Presenters:
- **Roderick Mitchell**, President, Bedford Stuyvesant Restoration Corporation
- **Karen Phillips**, Chief Executive Officer, Abyssinian Development Corporation

Reaction Panel:
How can Saint Paul strengthen neighborhood based economic development?
- **Paul Fate**, Senior Program Director, Local Initiatives Support Corporation
- **Rev. James Battle**, Mount Olivet Baptist Church
- **Denise Miller**, Executive Director, PROCEED

Saint Paul: Putting It All Together

Tuesday, June 17
Public Forum 5:30 - 8:30
Gustavus Adolphus Lutheran Church, Arcade at Larpenteur

Purpose: To promote dialogue and foster innovations in our community economic development efforts in Saint Paul.

In this session we will:
- **Synthesize** learning from the previous three forums featuring Chattanooga, Bedford Stuyvesant and Harlem, and San Antonio
- **Explore** examples of community economic development efforts from Saint Paul

Agendas for each forum:
5:00-5:30 Registration
5:30-6:00 Buffet dinner
6:00-8:30 Presentations and audience discussion

Please note:
- All events are free and open to the public, but advanced registration is required for dinners.
- Use the form below to register. Call 642 2083 for information.

Please register for any or all of the sessions. Advanced registration is required for dinner. Attend all four, if you can!

☐ **Chattanooga: The Power of Leaders**
Thursday, April 3

☐ **Brooklyn & Harlem: Creating Marketplaces**
Tuesday, April 29

☐ **San Antonio:**
Project QUEST — Inspired Workforce Development
Thursday, May 29

☐ **Saint Paul: Putting It All Together**
Tuesday, June 17

Type or print the information requested OR attach your business card(s). Please make as many copies of this form as you need.

Name _____

Organization/Group _____

Address _____

City/State/Zip _____

Phone _____

Send registrations to Cities at Work 2, Attn: Kate Murphy, 919 Lafond Avenue, Saint Paul, MN 55104-2198. Fax number: 642 2088

Unleashing the Power of Our Community

A Public Dialogue on Race, Connections, and Commitment

Cities at Work 1999—Spring Forums

Stop Talking, Just Do It!
Saint Paul Youth's Perspectives on Bridging Differences

JOIN Michael Pritchard, humorist and youth advocate, for a lively and provocative "talk show" discussion with Saint Paul youth about the daily realities of living in a multicultural world.

GAIN INSIGHT into how we as a community can learn from—and use—the experiences and perspectives of our youth.

EXPLORE new ways to involve youth in creating collaborative solutions for Saint Paul's future.

Wednesday, April 28, 1999
Public Forum: 5:00-8:30 p.m.
Arlington High School
1459 Rice Street

Moderated by Yusef Mgeni
The Urban Coalition

Face-to-Face
How We Interact

EXPERIENCE the raw poetry, powerful memories, and some funny, yet brave stories told by those who have left behind their homes and culture to create a new life for themselves and their families in Minnesota.

EXPLORE the ways to break through the barriers of culture, communication, and perceptions to build a vibrant Saint Paul.

SHARE food and conversation while learning how to foster cross-cultural understanding and nurture relationships in our increasingly diverse communities.

Tuesday, May 18, 1999
Public Forum: 5:00-8:30 p.m.
Bandana Banquet and Conference Center
Bandana Square (near Energy Park Drive and Lexington Avenue)

Moderated by Yusef Mgeni
The Urban Coalition
Featuring an original performance by Illusion Theater

Cities at Work 1999—Fall Forums

Changing the Way We Do Business
Date and location to be determined

Citizens, nonprofits, neighborhood groups, and businesses in Saint Paul are increasingly working in multi-sector and multicultural groups and partnerships to accomplish both mutual benefit and shared goals for our community. At this forum, we will explore leadership and participation in multicultural decision-making settings and collaborative ventures. We will identify ways to utilize our differences to achieve common purpose, shared commitment, and greater community impact.

Beyond Tolerance
A Call to Action
Date and location to be determined

The final *Cities at Work* forum will generate ideas for taking positive steps to engage Saint Paul as a community in nurturing our diversity, promoting reconciliation, and dismantling racism.

We will explore individual actions that can make a difference, learn how to get involved with groups or organizations already initiating change, and identify community-wide strategies and approaches.

Community Circle Dialogues

What are community circle dialogues?
Small, diverse discussion groups that meet for five, two-hour sessions over a period of two months for honest and open dialogue. The discussions are led by trained facilitators and a written study guide to explore the challenges of housing, education, race, and multiculturalism in Saint Paul.

What is the purpose of the community circle dialogues?
Community circle dialogues build a greater understanding of other viewpoints and encourage individuals and communities to take action and promote public policy change.

How can I get involved?
The community circle dialogues are being sponsored by community-based organizations, schools, and local businesses throughout Saint Paul and the broader metropolitan region. For more information about how you or your organization can participate, call 651-659-6031.

Cities at Work 1999 Sponsors and Funders
Amherst H. Wilder Foundation • Asian Pacific Endowment for Community Development • Catholic Charities • City Solutions • East Side Neighborhood Development/VISTA • Education and Housing Equity Project/Community Circles Collaborative • Jane Addams School for Democracy • Local Initiatives Support Corporation • MRA Initiatives for Change - Twin Cities • Minnesota Alliance with Youth • National Conference for Community and Justice • Otto Bremer Foundation • St. Paul Council of Churches • St. Paul/Ramsey Children's Initiative • St. Paul Planning Commission • The Roy Wilkins Center for Human Relations and Social Justice/Humphrey Institute of Public Affairs • United Way of the St. Paul Area • The Urban Coalition • YMCA of Greater St. Paul • And a diverse group of community volunteers

Agendas for Each Forum
5:00-5:30 p.m. Registration and buffet dinner
5:30-8:30 p.m. Program and audience discussion
All events are free and open to the public, but advanced registration is required for dinner. For more information, contact Kate at 651-642-2083 or kmm@wilder.org

Registration
Please use this form to register for the first two Cities at Work forums. Advanced registration is required for dinner.

Please check the forum(s) you plan to attend:

☐ **Stop Talking, Just Do It!**
Saint Paul Youth's Perspectives on Bridging Differences
Wednesday, April 28, 5:00-8:30 p.m.

☐ **Face-to-Face**
How We Interact
Tuesday, May 18, 5:00-8:30 p.m.

Name _____

Organization (if any) _____

Address _____

City _____ State _____ Zip _____

Phone _____ Fax _____ Email _____

Send completed forms to: Kate Murphy, Wilder Foundation, 919 Lafond Avenue, Saint Paul, MN 55104 OR fax: 651-642-2088

Cities at Work 1999

Unleashing the Power of Our Community

A Public Dialogue on Race, Connections, and Commitment

Worksheets

Electronic versions of these worksheets may be downloaded from the publisher's web site. Use the following URL to obtain the worksheets.

http://www.wilder.org/pubs/workshts/pubs_worksheets1.html?069318

The online worksheets are intended for use in the same way as photocopies of the worksheets, but they are in a form that allows you to type in your responses and reformat the worksheets to fit your community forum work. Please do not download the worksheets unless you or your organization has purchased this field guide.

Use this worksheet to help you plan your forum.

The timeline below is appropriate for a large community forum and can be used as part of the planning and monitoring for the event. If the forum is small, the timeline might be shorter, but don't underestimate the time planning will take.

Seven to eight months before the forum

- ❑ Identify the need for a forum
- ❑ Recruit a strong planning group
- ❑ Hold the first planning group meeting
- ❑ Shape the goals and design and determine target audience
- ❑ Conduct relevant research and identify current literature
- ❑ Draft a budget
- ❑ Draft a concept paper
- ❑ Recruit sponsors
- ❑ Solicit funders for financial support

Six months before the forum

- ❑ Hold the second planning group meeting
- ❑ Set forum date (research potential conflicts)
- ❑ Survey facilities available in the community
- ❑ Choose evaluation methods
- ❑ Draft agenda
- ❑ Brainstorm a list of possible speakers and research them

Five months before the forum

- ❑ Hold the third planning group meeting
- ❑ Approach potential speakers, facilitators
- ❑ Confirm and contract with speakers
- ❑ Reserve and contract with facility for forum

- ❑ Plan publicity campaign, including brochures, posters, press releases
- ❑ Build database, soliciting addresses for target audience from planning group
- ❑ Plan forum packets and order office supplies and any published materials
- ❑ Establish billing processes
- ❑ Continue to research literature and prepare summaries of information

Four months before the forum

- ❑ Draft brochure or invitation text
- ❑ Secure photographer, graphic designer, and printer for publicity materials
- ❑ Establish registration process
- ❑ Form relationships with media
- ❑ Draft press releases for daily and weekly newspapers, newsletters, and so forth
- ❑ Recruit freelance writer for opinion piece
- ❑ Draft menu and research possible caterers

Three months before the forum

- ❑ Hold the fourth planning group meeting
- ❑ Print brochures and posters and prepare for mailing
- ❑ Broadcast e-mail announcements
- ❑ Send public service announcements to radio or TV stations
- ❑ Create evaluation forms

- Recruit sponsors for follow-up action
- Work out audiovisual equipment details with facility and technicians
- Fine-tune agenda and obtain biographical information from speakers
- Select menu and caterer
- Reconnect with speakers

Two months before the forum

- Mail or distribute brochures, invitations, and targeted promotions
- Review facility setup, equipment needs, and food details with facility
- Contract with caterers if necessary
- Finalize style of forum, including registration packet materials, nametags, signage
- Begin processing registrations

One month before the forum

- Reserve time for fifth planning group meeting (if needed)
- Reconfirm details and changes with facility and audiovisual technician
- Reconfirm with caterer (if used)
- Send press releases to daily and weekly newspapers
- Ensure flyers and posters are distributed and posted
- Recruit volunteers to help on the day of the forum (registration, greeting, decoration, hosting speakers, cleanup, and so forth)
- Assemble masters for registration packet
- Mail reminder postcards, e-mails, and so forth

Two weeks before the forum

- Send logistics information, program brochure, and travel and pickup details to speakers
- Confirm and orient volunteers on assigned tasks
- Call caterer with number attending forum

One week before the forum

- Assemble forum registration packets, prepare signage and nametags, review supplies needed for forum and registration area
- Call speakers for last-minute details
- Check equipment, get keys for facility (if necessary)
- Review the Forum Checklist.

The day of the forum

- Check on facility and breakout room setup
- Conduct facilitator training (if planned for just before the forum)
- Check on last-minute catering issues
- Prepare registration table and materials (see checklist)
- Post signage
- Welcome speakers to forum (pick them up at the airport if necessary)
- Launch the forum!

Use this budget worksheet as a guide in developing a budget for your forum. Your budget line items may be different from the ones in this worksheet.

Instructions

- Identify your budget assumptions, such as probable keynote speaker costs, location costs, advertising costs, and so forth. These will become clearer as your planning group's forum concept begins to take shape.
- After each planning group meeting, revise and add to the budget based on the group's input.
- When the budget is completed, format it into a document that can be used for potential funders or sponsors.

1. **Budget Assumptions** _____

   _____

   _____

   _____

2. **Revenue and Expense Budgets**

REVENUE		Totals
Grants		$
Partner Contributions		$
_____ Partners @ $_____ =	$	
_____ Partners @ $_____ =	$	
In-kind Contributions		$
Donated _____ =	$	
Donated _____ =	$	
Donated _____ =	$	
Participant Fees		$
_____ Registrants @ $_____ =	$	
TOTAL REVENUE		$

EXPENSE	Totals
Salary/Benefits	$ _____
Forum coordinator:____ FTE for ____ months = $ _____	
Admin. support: ____ FTE for ____ months = $ _____	
Contractor Fees	$ _____
Speakers: ____ @ $_____/day = $ _____	
Translators (if used) = $ _____	
Graphic design = $ _____	
Photographer for brochure = $ _____	
Photographer for day of forum = $ _____	
Facilitators: _____ @ $_____ = $ _____	
Research = $ _____	
Printing and Copying	$ _____
Brochure = $ _____	
Miscellaneous copying: _____copies @ $_____ = $ _____	
Postage	$ _____
Bulk: _____ pieces @ $_____ = $ _____	
First class: _____ pieces @ $_____ = $ _____	
Courier: _____ @ $_____ = $ _____	
Mail house (if used) = $	
Other Promotional Materials	$ _____
Purchase ads in newspapers, etc. = $ _____	
Travel for Presenters	$ _____
Airfare: ____ trips @ $_____ = $ _____	
Taxis: ____ trips @ $_____ = $ _____	
Room/Board for Presenters	$ _____
_____ days @ $ _____/day = $ _____	
Program/Office Supplies	$ _____
Food	$ _____
Forum food: _____ people @ $_____ = $ _____	
Planning meetings:	
____ people x ____ meetings @ $_____ = $ _____	
Facilitator/volunteer training = $ _____	
Room/Equipment Rental	$ _____
Room rental = $ _____	
Equipment: = $ _____	
Subtotal	$ _____
Overhead	$ _____
TOTAL EXPENSE	$ _____

Use this worksheet as a guide to help you develop a concept paper for your forum.

Instructions
- Outline ideas for the forum prior to your first planning group meeting.
- After the first meeting of the planning group, prepare a draft of the concept paper.
- Refer to the sample concept paper in Appendix A to see how each section could be written.
- After each planning group meeting, revise and add to the concept paper based on the group's input.
- When the draft is final, format it into a document that can be used for potential funders or sponsors.

1. **Background**
   Why do you want to hold a forum? What conditions make the forum goals timely or urgent?

2. **Goals**
   What do you want your forum to accomplish? What outcomes will result?

3. **Target audience**
   Who will benefit from the forum? Whom should you invite?

4. **Design elements**
   What events will your forum include? What other activities will be needed (research, focus groups, promotion, follow-up activities) to make your forum a success? When would be the best time to hold this forum?

5. **Planning group**
   Who will be on your planning group? What are their affiliations—both through their work and within the community?

6. **Sponsorship**
   Who will the forum sponsors be? What kind of commitment will sponsors make?

7. **Staffing**
   Who will staff your forum, including support for the planning group, promotions, registration, and other logistics? Will one organization serve as fiscal agent?

8. **Evaluation**
    How will you evaluate the effectiveness of your forum in achieving its goals?

9. **Cost**
    What will the forum and related activities cost? Provide a summary in the body of
    the concept paper, and attach a complete operating budget for potential funders.

10. **Funding plans**
    How, and from whom, will you raise money and in-kind contributions to support
    your forum?

Use this worksheet to get an accurate picture of who will be sponsoring your forum, how they want to be presented, and what their commitments are as sponsors.

Instructions
- Adapt the choices regarding sponsor involvement to fit your forum situation.
- Make copies of this worksheet and distribute to individuals and organizations that you would like as sponsors of your forum. Ask them to complete the worksheet and return it by a specific date.
- When you have collected worksheets from all of your potential sponsors, add appropriate names to your concept paper.

The effectiveness and success of this forum depend on the participation of many individuals and organizations in the community. This checklist will help us get a picture of who wants to be involved, and how.

Your organization or company _____
(As you would like it to appear on promotional materials)

Name of contact: _____

Phone: _____

E-mail:_____

Please check off as many boxes as you can commit to. If not yourself, indicate who from your agency will be the contact for specific activities listed below.

❑　Be a sponsoring organization or company. Sponsors will have their name on all promotional materials and will be acknowledged at all the forums. Sponsors will
- Participate regularly in planning meetings, working on at least one committee.
- Help distribute promotional information through direct mailings, providing mailing labels, putting announcements in newsletters, sending letters to constituents, or calling community leaders.
- Make a contribution (optional):
  ____ Sponsor a lunch forum ($600–$1,000).
  ____ Contribute money to cover forum expenses. Amount: _____
  ____ In-kind contributions (printing, brochure design, mailing, food).
  Please specify: _____

❑   Serve on the planning committee with or without a sponsorship commitment.

❑   Work on a subcommittee:
    ___ Fundraising subcommittee (approximately four meetings)

    ___ Advocacy subcommittee (approximately four meetings)

    ___ Marketing and promotions subcommittee (approximately four meetings)

    ___ Event planning and logistics subcommittee (approximately four meetings)

❑   Provide _____(#) facilitators for small group discussions at the forum (involves a one-hour training session and attendance at the forum, and ideally should be people with facilitation experience and skills).

❑   Help out at the forum:
    ___ Registration table

    ___ Setup/decorations

    ___ Cleanup

❑   Will sponsor follow-up action by providing:
    ___ Meeting space

    ___ Printing/copying of materials

    ___ Child care for participants

    ___ Funding for _____

Use this worksheet to evaluate facilities you are considering for the forum.

Instructions
- Fill out one worksheet for each facility under consideration.
- Share results with the planning group to decide on which facility to use.

1. **Facility name and location**
    What is the correct address? Does the facility have a map to its location?

2. **Contact person/phone**
    Whom should we contact with questions? Will a contact person be on-site (janitor, audio-video technician, staff)? If yes, what is the fee?

3. **Room capacity**
    How many people will the room hold seated at tables?
    Seated auditorium style?

4. **Breakout rooms**
    How many breakout rooms are available? Where are the breakout rooms? How big are they? Are they equipped with tables, chairs, flip chart, and markers?

5. **Fees**
    What is the charge for rental of each space used? Is there a parking fee? What is the charge for audiovisual equipment?

6. **Handicap accessible**
    Are the rooms, bathrooms, and parking handicap accessible?

7. **Parking**
    Where is the parking? Will it accommodate the number of people expected? What is the cost?

8. **Style and capacity of tables**

How many tables and how many chairs are available? What kind of tables are they? (For example, do you need round tables that seat eight or rectangular tables that seat ten?)

9. **Food service or catering**

Is there a kitchen that we can use? Are there any restrictions in using an outside caterer? If we will be serving liquor, does the facility have restrictions? Do we need a liquor license?

10. **Audiovisual equipment**

Is there a podium or stage for speakers? What kind of audiovisual equipment is available (projectors, screens, lighting, public address system, microphones, and so forth)?

11. **Insurance**

Does the facility have insurance to cover this event or will we need to purchase our own?

12. Setup and cleanup

What do we need to do and what will the facility staff do (set up and tear down tables and chairs, clear tables, and so forth)?

13. Room decorations and signage

Are there any restrictions on putting up decorations or signage?

14. Room setup

Diagram the desired room setup, including table and chair placement, food-service flow, and location of microphones, registration table, and exhibit spaces.

Helpful Resources

Books, Articles, Organizations, and Web Sites

Books

Avner, Marcia. *The Lobbying and Advocacy Handbook for Nonprofit Organizations: Shaping Public Policy at the State and Local Level.* Saint Paul, MN: Amherst H. Wilder Foundation, 2002.

Ayre, Darvin, Gruffie Clough, and Tyler Norris. *Facilitating Community Change.* Boulder, CO: Grove Consultants International, 2000.

Bryson, John M., and Barbara C. Crosby. *Leadership for the Common Good: Tackling Public Problems in a Shared-Power World.* San Francisco: Jossey-Bass, 1992.

Chrislip, David D., and Carl E. Larson. *Collaborative Leadership: How Citizens and Civic Leaders Can Make a Difference.* San Francisco: Jossey-Bass, 1994.

Creighton, James L. *Involving Citizens in Community Decision Making: A Guidebook.* Washington, DC: Creighton & Creighton, Inc., Program for Community Problem Solving, 1992.

Emery, Merrelyn, and Ron Purser. *Search Conferences in Action.* San Francisco: Jossey-Bass, 1996.

Hamaker, Molly Roth, and Cynthia Cusick. *Town Meeting Tool Kit.* Brattleboro, VT: Center for Living Democracy, 1993.

Hinds, Michael deCourcy. *A Nice Place to Live: Creating Communities, Fighting Sprawl.* Prepared by Public Agenda. Dubuque, IA: Kendall/Hunt, 1999.

———. *Racial and Ethnic Tensions: What Should We Do?* Washington, DC: National Issues Forums Institute, 2000.

Holman, Peggy, and Tom Devane (Eds.). *The Change Handbook: Group Methods for Shaping the Future.* San Francisco: Berrett-Koehler, 1999.

Kennedy, Debbe. *Action Dialogues: Meaningful Conversations to Accelerate Change (Diversity Breakthrough! Strategic Action Series).* San Francisco: Berrett-Koehler, 2000.

Lappe, Frances Moore, and Paul Martin DuBois. *The Quickening America: Rebuilding Our Nation, Remaking Our Lives.* San Francisco: Jossey-Bass, 1994.

Lukas, Carol A. *Consulting with Nonprofits: A Practitioner's Guide.* Saint Paul, MN: Amherst H. Wilder Foundation, 1998.

Mathews, David, and Noelle McAfee. *Making Choices Together: The Power of Public Deliberation.* Dayton, OH: Charles F. Kettering Foundation, 1997.

Mattessich, Paul, and Barbara Monsey. *Community Building: What Makes It Work.* Saint Paul, MN: Amherst H. Wilder Foundation, 1997.

McGill, Ian, and Liz Beaty. *Action Learning: A Guide for Professional, Management and Educational Development,* 2nd ed. London: Kogan Page; Sterling, VA: Stylus Publications, 2001.

McKnight, John L., and John P. Kretzmann. *Building Communities from the Inside Out: A Path Toward Finding and Mobilizing a Community's Assets.* Evanston, IL: Institute for Policy Research, 1993.

Minnesota Parenting Association. *Hopes & Dreams, Challenges & Strengths: Minnesota Parents Talk about What Their Families Value.* Saint Paul, MN: Minnesota Parenting Association, 1998.

Nagle, Ami. *A Seat at the Table: Keeping the "Public" in Public Policy.* Washington, DC: Neighborhood Funders Group, Issue Brief, 2001.

Norris, Tyler, and Linda Howell. *Healthy People in Healthy Communities: A Dialogue Guide.* Chicago: Coalition for Healthier Cities and Communities, 1999.

Parachini, Larry, and Sally Covington. *Community Organizing Toolbox: A Funder's Guide to Community Organizing.* Washington, DC: Neighborhood Funders Group, 2001.

Poupart, John. *To Build a Bridge: Working with American Indian Communities.* Saint Paul, MN: American Indian Policy Center, 2000.

Putnam, Robert D. *Bowling Alone: The Collapse and Revival of American Community.* New York: Simon & Schuster, 2000.

Rhein, Michael; et al. *Advancing Community Public Health Systems in the 21st Century: Emerging Strategies and Innovations from the Turning Point Experience.* Washington, DC: National Association of County and City Health Officials (NACCHO), 2001.

Richards, Audrey (Ed.). *Successful Seminars, Conferences and Workshops.* San Francisco: Public Management Institute, 1980.

Scully, Patrick, and Matt Leighninger (Eds.). *Smart Talk for Growing Communities: Meeting the Challenges of Growth and Development.* Pomfret, CT: Topsfield Foundation, 1998.

————. *Toward a More Perfect Union in an Age of Diversity: A Guide to Building Stronger Communities Through Public Dialogue.* Pomfret, CT: Topsfield Foundation, 1998.

Simon, Judith Sharken. *The Wilder Nonprofit Field Guide to Conducting Successful Focus Groups.* Saint Paul, MN: Amherst H. Wilder Foundation, 1999.

SRI International. *We Did It Ourselves: Guidelines for Successful Community Collaboration.* Sacramento, CA: Sierra Health Foundation, 2000.

Stanfield, Brian (Ed.). *The Art of Focused Conversation.* Toronto, Ontario, Canada: Canadian Institute of Cultural Affairs, 1997.

Stern, Gary J. *Marketing Workbook for Nonprofit Organizations Volume I: Develop the Plan,* 2nd ed. Saint Paul, MN: Amherst H. Wilder Foundation, 2001.

Stone, Rebecca, and Benjamin Butler. *Core Issues in Comprehensive Community-Building Initiatives: Exploring Power and Race.* Chicago: University of Chicago, Chapin Hall Center for Children, 2000.

Wallach, Lawrence; et al. *News for a Change: An Advocate's Guide to Working with the Media.* Thousand Oaks, CA: Sage Publications, 1999.

Wells, Lloyd P., and Larry Lemmel. *Recreating Democracy: Breathing New Life into American Communities.* Woolwich, ME: Center for Consensual Democracy, 2000.

Articles

Emery, Merrelyn. "The Power of Community Search Conferences." *Journal for Quality and Participation* (December 1995): 70–79.

Herman, Melanie. "How Risky Is Your Special Event?" *Nonprofit World* (January/February 2002): 18–19.

Johnson, Neal (Ed.). "Talk Show Democracy." *The Public Innovator: A Bulletin for Change Agents* (October 1994): 1–7.

Nee, David. "Engaging the Community: Constituency Building at the Graustein Memorial Fund." *Insight* 3, no. 12 (Fall 2000): 17.

Sharp, Marcia, and Ann Beaudry. "Communications as Engagement." *The Millennium Report* (November 1994): 1–10.

Weiss, Mary. "Sustaining Large Systems Change." *Consulting Today* (Spring 2000): 4.

York, Virginia. "Panama City Forums Link Citizens and Officeholders." *Connections* (June 1997): 3–4.

Organizations and Web sites

Charles F. Kettering Foundation
200 Commons Road
Dayton, OH 45459
Web site: www.kettering.org

Publishes forum discussion guides through National Issues Forums including guides on affirmative action, drugs, economy, education, family, foreign policy, freedom of speech, healthcare, immigration, justice system, natural resources, politics, poverty, racial inequality, social security, and violence. Publications include

- *Connections,* a newsletter of the Charles F. Kettering Foundation, Order Department, P.O. Box 41626, Dayton, OH 45441, 800-600-4060
- *Kettering Review,* a newsletter of the Charles F. Kettering Foundation, 937-434-7300

Dialogue to Action Initiative
P.O. Box 402
Brattleboro, VT 05302
Web site: www.thatway.org/dialogue

Provides forum to keep leaders informed, involved, and inspired. Uses the dialogue process for peace building, improving intergroup relations, fostering innovation, influencing policy, educating citizens, and transforming conflicts.

International Association for Public Participation
11166 Huron Street, Suite 27
Denver, CO 80234
Web site: www.iap2.org

Promotes and improves the practice of public participation in relation to individuals, governments, institutions, and other entities that affect the public interest in nations throughout the world.

National Issues Forums Institute
P.O. Box 75306
Washington, DC 20013
Web site: www.nifi.org

Nationwide network of educational and community organizations that deliberate about nationwide issues. Provides the "National Issues Starter Kit," which includes the Public Policy Institute Guide, a summary of NIF's discussion guides, a moderator guide, and a network contact list. Downloadable at http://www.nifi.org/starter.html.

Public Conversations Project
46 Kondazian Street
Watertown, MA 02472
Web site: www.publicconversations.org

Promotes constructive conversations and relationships among people and groups that have differing values, worldviews, and perspectives about divisive public issues. Provides *Constructive Conversations about Challenging Times: A Guide to Community Dialogue,* a downloadable resource for people who want to conduct constructive conversations with neighbors, colleagues, and fellow worshippers about the September 11 attacks and their aftermath.

Renewing Democracy through Interracial/Multicultural Community Building
School of Politics & Economics - Institute for Democratic Renewal
McManus 225
170 East Tenth Street
Claremont, CA 91711

A national project by distinguished individuals who have devoted themselves to community building and racial and cultural reconciliation work. Provides *A Community Builder's Tool Kit: 15 Tools for Creating Healthy, Productive, Interracial/Multicultural Communities*. This primer for revitalizing democracy from the ground up can be downloaded at www.race-democracy.org/toolkit.html.

Study Circles Resource Center
P.O. Box 203
Pomfret, CT 06258
Web site: www.studycircles.org

Produces resource material and training for individuals and communities that want to initiate study circles. Provides forum discussion guides on building strong neighborhoods, immigration and race, jobs, education, violence, youth, and other topics.

Civic Practices Network (CPN)
Center for Human Resources
Heller School for Advanced Studies in Social Welfare
Brandeis University
60 Turner Street
Waltham, MA 02154
Web site: www.cpn.org

This web site includes "The Electronic Forum Handbook: Study Circles in Cyberspace" at http://www.cpn.org/tools/manuals/Networking/studycircles.html

This handbook documents the results of moderators trained in face-to-face dialogue who experimented with an electronic version on the Internet. Two classes—one at Ithaca College in New York and one at the University of Georgia—were paired for an electronic dialogue experience in 1994. The handbook is based in part on Study Circles Resource Center materials.

Forum Design Elements

Following are techniques, tools, and activities frequently used in forums. Information about these and other forum design options can be found in the resources listed in this appendix.

Brainstorming is used to come up with a large number of ideas in a short amount of time. The facilitator of a brainstorming session starts by establishing ground rules, including (1) come up with as many ideas as possible; (2) all ideas are good ones; and (3) don't judge or criticize any idea, or mention that it has already been said. Brainstorming can be used for a brief, small group discussion or for a longer, large group discussion.

Dialogue is a highly structured discussion of deeply held feelings and beliefs on a given topic. Common ground rules of dialogue include (1) listen carefully, (2) speak honestly, and (3) be brief. Training is necessary to make this process work effectively.

Panel Presentations are often used at forums to quickly get a variety of opinions or positions on a topic. They can be the main presentation, or they can be a reaction to a presentation. Panelists are often chosen for their diverse views and representation, and they are usually given a limited amount of time (up to five minutes) to speak. A skilled moderator manages time limits and fields questions.

Simulations and Role Plays are used to make discussions and ideas as real and personal as possible. They are structured exercises that put people into a real-life situation. Learning occurs as participants reflect on their experience in the role play. Simulations and role plays require careful planning and skilled facilitation.

Talk Show is a variation on the panel presentation model, often using a more informal setting or livelier format. It requires a moderator with a somewhat theatrical or entertaining style.

Town Meetings refer to public gatherings to solicit a wide range of opinions on a topic. Normally the meeting begins with the presentation of information, often noting pros and cons on an issue. Audience members then step up to a microphone and respond with their opinions on the issue.

Visioning is a structured discussion process used to create a picture of what a neighborhood, community, or city might look like in the future. It is often used as part of lengthier planning processes. As part of visioning sessions, people might be asked to identify what they would like to see in the future, what barriers are blocking them from realizing their vision, and what changes or steps would help them move toward making the vision a reality.

Typical discussion questions for a community visioning forum include the following:

- What is your dream for our community? What kind of community (or school, neighborhood, and so forth) do you want to see in the future?
- What do you see as our community's major assets or strengths?
- What is blocking us from reaching our vision? What are the barriers that may keep us from being successful?
- What do you want to change?
- What are three ways we might begin making progress toward achieving this dream?

Learning circles, open space technology, and search conferences, described below, are stand-alone design elements, and are not usually combined with other elements.

Learning Circles, also called study circles, are small groups of eight to twelve people who meet over a one- to two-month period to learn about a particular issue or topic. Learning circles can be used prior to a public forum to prepare people for deeper discussion on an issue. Normally a trained facilitator and well-researched study guide are provided to each study circle.

Open Space Technology is used to discuss and explore issues in a system or community. It is the least structured of techniques for working with large groups. The large group creates the agenda and forms interest groups around topics. Open space meetings usually last one to three days and require skilled, experienced facilitators.

Search Conferences, or *Future Search Workshops,* are relatively long sessions, usually three days, used to create a plan for the future and build the capacity of a system or community. They are used to facilitate large, diverse groups through fast-track planning and to keep critical choices in the hands of participants. These events require trained facilitators with experience in design and orchestration of search conferences or future search workshops.

Forum Checklist

The following checklist provides a format to organize forum logistics. Depending on the design of the forum, not all of the items in the checklist will apply. Also, in some areas, the checklist gives more detail; in others, you will need to look in the book for guidance and details.

Task	Date complete	Who is responsible
Plan the forum and obtain resources		
Recruit forum planning group		
Set up database for planning group		
Decide forum topics and target audience		
Determine overall forum series design		
Determine individual forum design		
Conduct research to gather accurate information		
Develop a budget		
Identify and recruit sponsors		
Select possible dates		
Create forum agenda		
Identify resource people		
Identify possible speakers		
Select speakers		
Confirm with speakers including: • Clarity on topics • Fees and billing process • Dates and daily schedule • Travel arrangements • Speaker handouts • Equipment needed • Biographical information		
Contract with speakers		
Arrange for transportation and lodging for speakers, if needed		

Task	Date complete	Who is responsible
Develop detailed internal agenda with times (share this with speakers, panelists, moderators, and so forth)		
Maintain ongoing communication with speakers		
Arrange fees and internal billing processes		
Conduct orientation for moderator and welcomer		
Recruit small group facilitators		
Organize facilitator training • Identify and recruit or hire trainers • Provide written instructions • Schedule training date and time • Identify training space		
Recruit community exhibitors, if appropriate		
Plan the evaluation process		
Handle registration materials and handout packets		
Registration: • Set up registration database; make sure speakers, planning group, and coordinator get registered in database • As event approaches, evaluate registration level and consider measures to increase registration if needed		
Identify and collect handout materials		
Create evaluation form		
Schedule volunteers or extra staff to cover: *Before the event:* • Packet preparation—copying and stuffing		

Task	Date complete	Who is responsible
Schedule volunteers or staff to cover: *At the event:* • Registration table • Food service • Cleanup • Collect evaluation forms from audience		
Order office supplies for forum day including: • Paper for handouts and agendas • Card stock for table tents • Clips/folders for packets • Markers for nametags—2 per table • Pens/pencils for registration table and audience tables—2 per table • Blank nametags for "walk-ins"		
Prepare for copying of handout materials • Prepare and approve sample packet • Reserve room to assemble packets • Arrange extra staff or volunteer support (or outsource to photo-copy business)		
Copy handout materials—prepare an additional 10 percent		
Assemble handout packets		
Prepare signage. Depending on forum design, you may need: • Table tents with the name of panelists • "Reserved table" signs or table numbers • Evaluation drop-off box • Registration table signs • Table discussion questions or visuals • Food labels (particularly to note vegetarian) • Speaker timing signs: 3 minutes, STOP • Directional event signs		

Task	Date complete	Who is responsible
Prepare maps to fax and over-the-phone directions to forum site		
Send confirmation postcards to registrants		
If registration is low, send reminder postcards to mail list		
Develop publicity and promotions		
Plan publicity and any direct mailings		
Assign responsibility for promotion follow-up		
Plan and purchase thank-you gifts for facilitators		
Request and collect mailing lists or labels from planning group and other interested people		
Personal letter invitations • Create invitation list • Identify logistics for invitation—Who drafts letter? Whose letterhead? Signatures? • Identify who receives the RSVPs		
Draft brochure • Identify graphic designer, editor, printer • Create draft copy • Work with designer to create final product		
Proofread and obtain final approval on brochure		
Send brochure to printer		
Make mailing labels		
Mail brochures; be sure they are in the hands of audience 6 weeks before the forum		
Create poster, single-page flyer, or fax information sheet		

Task	Date complete	Who is responsible
Establish media relations		
Draft press releases, media advisories		
Create media contact list; print labels		
Write up talking points		
Recruit writers for opinion pieces		
Create display ad copy for neighborhood newspapers, organization newsletters, e-mail		
Coordinate press interviews with major speakers		
Hire photographer		
Arrange for audiovisual taping, if desired		
Handle facility and food logistics		
Identify site needs and preferences		
Research possible sites and reserve potential spaces while date is being selected		
Confirm with site when date is determined; cancel reservations with unused sites (remember you may need them next time!)		
Make equipment and audiovisual arrangements		
Determine room setup		
Select caterer and menu • Will caterer deliver? Extra fee for delivery? • When can we give a final count for attendees? • What will we do with leftover food? (Contact food bank to research.) • Make sure caterer has directions to site, if needed • Double-check everything		
Decide on room decorations		

Task	Date complete	Who is responsible
Things to bring on the day of the event		
Handout packets		
Nametags, table tents, signs		
Registration list		
Blank sign-in sheets for walk-ins		
Supply box—tape, blank signs, markers, scissors		
Flip charts and markers		
Dinner supplies		
Water pitcher and glasses for speakers		
Audiovisual equipment (extension cords)		
Evaluation collection box		
Things to check on-site		
Last-minute catering issues		
Check room setup—is it all as requested? • Audiovisual equipment (it's there, it works) • Stage area (including podium, table and chairs for panelists) • Tables in place (food, registration, extra handout/information tables, exhibit tables, reserved table in audience for speakers/panelists) • Breakout rooms or areas set up as requested • Coat racks are in place		
Put up directional and facility signs		
Make sure you know . . . • How to adjust lights and where the outlets are • How to get help with audiovisual or building issues		

Task	Date complete	Who is responsible
Forum follow-up		
Complete attendance statistics • How many registered and attended • How many walk-ins		
Process invoices for . . . • Facility • Honoraria for speakers • Hotel and travel costs for speakers • Caterer(s) • Facilitators • Photographer		
Compile evaluation results		
Mail thank-you letters to speakers, panelists, facilitators, volunteers		
Conduct planning group debriefing—what worked, what didn't, and where do we go from here?		
Organize leftover materials		
Clean hard copy and computer files for future reference • Keep file copies of brochures • Keep originals of handouts • Keep a couple sample packets		

More results-oriented books
from the Amherst H. Wilder Foundation

For current prices, a free catalog, or to order call TOLL-FREE ☎ 800-274-6024

or visit us ONLINE at 🖥 www.wilder.org/pubs

Collaboration

Collaboration Handbook
Creating, Sustaining, and Enjoying the Journey
by Michael Winer and Karen Ray

Shows you how to get a collaboration going, set goals, determine everyone's roles, create an action plan, and evaluate the results. Includes a case study of one collaboration from start to finish, helpful tips on how to avoid pitfalls, and worksheets to keep everyone on track.

192 pages, softcover   Item # 069032

Collaboration: What Makes It Work, 2nd Ed.
by Paul Mattessich, PhD, Marta Murray-Close, BA, and Barbara Monsey, MPH

An in-depth review of current collaboration research. Major findings are summarized, critical conclusions are drawn, and twenty key factors influencing successful collaborations are identified. Includes The Wilder Collaboration Factors Inventory, which groups can use to assess their collaboration.

104 pages, softcover   Item # 069326

The Nimble Collaboration
Fine-Tuning Your Collaboration for Lasting Success
by Karen Ray

Shows you ways to make your existing collaboration more responsive, flexible, and productive. Provides three key strategies to help your collaboration respond quickly to changing environments and participants.

136 pages, softcover   Item # 069288

Funder's Guides

Community Visions, Community Solutions
Grantmaking for Comprehensive Impact
by Joseph A. Connor and Stephanie Kadel-Taras

Helps foundations, community funds, government agencies, and other grantmakers uncover a community's highest aspiration for itself, and support and sustain strategic efforts to get to workable solutions.

128 pages, softcover   Item # 06930X

Strengthening Nonprofit Performance
A Funder's Guide to Capacity Building
by Paul Connolly and Carol Lukas

This practical guide synthesizes the most recent capacity building practice and research into a collection of strategies, steps, and examples that you can use to get started on or improve funding to strengthen nonprofit organizations.

176 pages, softcover   Item # 069377

Management & Planning

Bookkeeping Basics
What Every Nonprofit Bookkeeper Needs to Know
by Debra L. Ruegg and Lisa M. Venkatrathnam

Complete with step-by-step instructions, a glossary of accounting terms, detailed examples, and handy reproducible forms, this book will enable you to successfully meet the basic bookkeeping requirements of your nonprofit organization—even if you have little or no formal accounting training.

128 pages, softcover   Item # 069296

Consulting with Nonprofits: A Practitioner's Guide
by Carol A. Lukas

A step-by-step, comprehensive guide for consultants. Addresses the art of consulting, how to run your business, and much more. Also includes tips and anecdotes from thirty skilled consultants.

240 pages, softcover   Item # 069172

The Wilder Nonprofit Field Guide to
Crafting Effective Mission and Vision Statements
by Emil Angelica

Guides you through two six-step processes that result in a mission statement, vision statement, or both. Shows how a clarified mission and vision lead to more effective leadership, decisions, fundraising, and management. Includes tips, sample statements, and worksheets.

88 pages, softcover   Item # 06927X

The Wilder Nonprofit Field Guide to Developing Effective Teams
by Beth Gilbertsen and Vijit Ramchandani

Helps you understand, start, and maintain a team. Provides tools and techniques for writing a mission statement, setting goals, conducting effective meetings, creating ground rules to manage team dynamics, making decisions in teams, creating project plans, and developing team spirit.

80 pages, softcover   Item # 069202

The Five Life Stages of Nonprofit Organizations
Where You Are, Where You're Going, and What to Expect When You Get There
by Judith Sharken Simon with J. Terence Donovan

Shows you what's "normal" for each development stage which helps you plan for transitions, stay on track, and avoid unnecessary struggles. This guide also includes The Wilder Nonprofit Life Stage Assessment. The Assessment allows you to plot and understand your organization's progress in seven arenas of organization development.

128 pages, softcover   Item # 069229

The Lobbying and Advocacy Handbook for Nonprofit Organizations
Shaping Public Policy at the State and Local Level
by Marcia Avner

The Lobbying and Advocacy Handbook is a planning guide and resource for nonprofit organizations that want to influence issues that matter to them. This book will help you decide whether to lobby and then put plans in place to make it work.

240 pages, softcover   Item # 069261

The Nonprofit Mergers Workbook
The Leader's Guide to Considering, Negotiating, and Executing a Merger
by David La Piana

A merger can be a daunting and complex process. Save time, money, and untold frustration with this highly practical guide that makes the process manageable and controllable. Includes case studies, decision trees, twenty-two worksheets, checklists, tips, and complete step-by-step guidance from seeking partners to writing the merger agreement, and more.

240 pages, softcover   Item # 069210

Resolving Conflict in Nonprofit Organizations
The Leader's Guide to Finding Constructive Solutions
by Marion Peters Angelica

Helps you identify conflict, decide whether to intervene, uncover and deal with the true issues, and design and conduct a conflict resolution process. Includes exercises to learn and practice conflict resolution skills, guidance on handling unique conflicts such as harassment and discrimination, and when (and where) to seek outside help with litigation, arbitration, and mediation.

192 pages, softcover   Item # 069164

Strategic Planning Workbook for Nonprofit Organizations, Revised and Updated
by Bryan Barry

Chart a wise course for your nonprofit's future. This time-tested workbook gives you practical step-by-step guidance, real-life examples, one nonprofit's complete strategic plan, and easy-to-use worksheets.

144 pages, softcover   Item # 069075

Marketing & Fundraising

The Wilder Nonprofit Field Guide to Conducting Successful Focus Groups
by Judith Sharken Simon

Shows how to collect valuable information without a lot of money or special expertise. Using this proven technique, you'll get essential opinions and feedback to help you check out your assumptions, do better strategic planning, improve services or products, and more.

80 pages, softcover   Item # 069199

Coping with Cutbacks:
The Nonprofit Guide to Success When Times Are Tight
by Emil Angelica and Vincent Hyman

Shows you practical ways to involve business, government, and other nonprofits to solve problems together. Also includes 185 cutback strategies you can put to use right away.

128 pages, softcover   Item # 069091

The Wilder Nonprofit Field Guide to Fundraising on the Internet
by Gary M. Grobman, Gary B. Grant, and Steve Roller

Your quick road map to using the Internet for fundraising. Shows you how to attract new donors, troll for grants, get listed on sites that assist donors, and learn more about the art of fundraising. Includes detailed reviews of 77 web sites useful to fundraisers, including foundations, charities, prospect research sites, and sites that assist donors.

64 pages, softcover   Item # 069180

Marketing Workbook for Nonprofit Organizations Volume I: Develop the Plan, 2nd Ed.
by Gary J. Stern

Don't just wish for results—get them! Here's how to create a straightforward, usable marketing plan. Includes the six P's of Marketing, how to use them effectively, a sample marketing plan, and detachable worksheets.

208 pages, softcover   Item # 069253

Marketing Workbook for Nonprofit Organizations Volume II: Mobilize People for Marketing Success
by Gary J. Stern

Put together a successful promotional campaign based on the most persuasive tool of all: personal contact. Learn how to mobilize your entire organization, its staff, volunteers, and supporters in a focused, one-to-one marketing campaign. Comes with *Pocket Guide for Marketing Representatives*. In it, your marketing representatives can record key campaign messages and find motivational reminders.

192 pages, softcover   Item # 069105

Venture Forth! The Essential Guide to Starting a Moneymaking Business in Your Nonprofit Organization
by Rolfe Larson

The most complete guide on nonprofit business development. Building on the experience of dozens of organizations, this handbook gives you a time-tested approach for finding, testing, and launching a successful nonprofit business venture.

272 pages, softcover   Item # 069245

Vital Communities

Community Building: What Makes It Work
by Wilder Research Center

Reveals twenty-eight keys to help you build community more effectively. Includes detailed descriptions of each factor, case examples of how they play out, and practical questions to assess your work.

112 pages, softcover   Item # 069121

Community Economic Development Handbook
by Mihailo Temali

A concrete, practical handbook to turning any neighborhood around. It explains how to start a community economic development organization, and then lays out the steps of four proven and powerful strategies for revitalizing inner-city neighborhoods.

288 pages, softcover   Item # 069369

Community Visions, Community Solutions
Grantmaking for Comprehensive Impact
See Funder's Guides

Violence Prevention & Intervention

The Little Book of Peace
Designed and illustrated by Kelly O. Finnerty

A pocket-size guide to help people think about violence and talk about it with their families and friends. You may download a free copy of The Little Book of Peace from our web site at www.wilder.org.

24 pages (minimum order 10 copies)   Item # 069083
*Also available in **Spanish** and **Hmong** language editions.*

Journey Beyond Abuse: A Step-by-Step Guide to Facilitating Women's Domestic Abuse Groups
by Kay-Laurel Fischer, MA, LP,
and Michael F. McGrane, LICSW

Create a program where women increase their understanding of the dynamics of abuse, feel less alone and isolated, and have a greater awareness of channels to safety. This book includes twenty-one group activities that you can combine to create groups of differing length and focus.

208 pages, softcover   Item # 069148

Moving Beyond Abuse: Stories and Questions for Women Who Have Lived with Abuse
(Companion guided journal to *Journey Beyond Abuse*)
A series of stories and questions that can be used in coordination with the sessions provided in the facilitator's guide or with the guidance of a counselor in other forms of support.

88 pages, softcover   Item # 069156

Foundations for Violence-Free Living: A Step-by-Step Guide to Facilitating Men's Domestic Abuse Groups
by David J. Mathews, MA, LICSW

A complete guide to facilitating a men's domestic abuse program. Includes twenty-nine activities, detailed guidelines for presenting each activity, and a discussion of psychological issues that may arise out of each activity.

240 pages, softcover   Item # 069059

On the Level

(Participant's workbook to *Foundations for Violence-Free Living*)

Contains forty-nine worksheets including midterm and final evaluations. Men can record their progress.

160 pages, softcover   Item # 069067

What Works in Preventing Rural Violence

by Wilder Research Center

An in-depth review of eighty-eight effective strategies you can use to prevent and intervene in violent behaviors, improve services for victims, and reduce repeat offenses. This report also includes a Community Report Card with step-by-step directions on how you can collect, record, and use information about violence in your community.

94 pages, softcover   Item # 069040

Ordering Information

Order by phone, fax or online

Call toll-free: 800-274-6024
Internationally: 651-659-6024

Fax: 651-642-2061

E-mail: books@wilder.org
Online: www.wilder.org/pubs

Mail: Amherst H. Wilder Foundation
Publishing Center
919 Lafond Avenue
St. Paul, MN 55104

Our NO-RISK guarantee

If you aren't completely satisfied with any book for any reason, simply send it back within 30 days for a full refund.

Pricing and discounts

For current prices and discounts, please visit our web site at www.wilder.org/pubs or call toll-free at 800-274-6024.

Do you have a book idea?

Wilder Publishing Center seeks manuscripts and proposals for books in the fields of nonprofit management and community development. To get a copy of our author guidelines, please call us at 800-274-6024. You can also download them from our web site at www.wilder.org/pubs/author_guide.html.

Visit us online

You'll find information about the Wilder Foundation and more details on our books, such as table of contents, pricing, discounts, endorsements, and more, at www.wilder.org/pubs.

Quality assurance

We strive to make sure that all the books we publish are helpful and easy-to-use. Our major workbooks are tested and critiqued by experts before being published. Their comments help shape the final book and—we trust—make it more useful to you.